Marx Hardy Montaigne Machiavelli Chesterton Joyce Austen
Defoe Abbott Melville Haggard Emerson Cooper Hugo Grimm
Stoker Carroll Christie Molière Eliot
Wilde Maupassant Byron Schiller
Garnett Einstein Fitzgerald Engels Smith Kafka Hall
Goethe Hawthorne Dostoyevsky Willis
Cotton Kipling Doyle
Baum Henry Nietzsche
Leslie Dumas Flaubert Turgenev Balzac
Stockton Vatsyayana Crane
Burroughs Verne
Curtis Tocqueville Gogol Vinci
Homer Widger Tolstoy Whitman Busch
Darwin Thoreau Twain Scott Plato Harte
Potter Freud Zola Lawrence Dickens Burton Hesse
Kant Jowett Stevenson
Andersen Cervantes
London Descartes Wells Voltaire Cooke
Poe Aristotle Burton
Hale James Hastings Irving
Bunner Shakespeare
Richter Chambers Irving
Doré Dante Chekhov da Shaw Wodehouse Benedict Alcott
Swift Pushkin
Newton

The Rural Life Problem of the United States Notes of an Irish Observer

Horace Curzon, Sir Plunkett

Imprint

This book is part of TREDITION CLASSICS

Author: Horace Curzon, Sir Plunkett
Cover design: Buchgut, Berlin – Germany

Publisher: tredition GmbH, Hamburg - Germany
ISBN: 978-3-8472-1471-7

www.tredition.com
www.tredition.de

THE RURAL LIFE PROBLEM

OF THE

UNITED STATES

THE MACMILLAN COMPANY
NEW YORK · BOSTON · CHICAGO
DALLAS · SAN FRANCISCO

MACMILLAN & CO., Limited
LONDON · BOMBAY · CALCUTTA
MELBOURNE

THE MACMILLAN CO. OF CANADA, Ltd.
TORONTO

[Pg iii]

THE

RURAL LIFE PROBLEM

OF THE

UNITED STATES

NOTES OF AN IRISH OBSERVER

BY

SIR HORACE PLUNKETT

New York
THE MACMILLAN COMPANY
1919

[Pg iv]

Norwood Press
J. S. Cushing Co. — Berwick & Smith Co.
Norwood, Mass., U.S.A.

[Pg v]

PREFATORY NOTE

The thoughts contained in the following pages relate to one side of the life of a country which has been to me, as to many Irishmen, a second home. They are offered in friendly recognition of kindness I cannot hope to repay, received largely as a student of American social and economic problems, from public-spirited Americans who, I know, will appreciate most highly any slight service to their country.

The substance of the book appeared in five articles contributed to the New York *Outlook* under the title "Conservation and Rural Life." Several American friends, deeply interested in the Rural Life problem, asked me to republish the series. In doing so, I have felt that I ought to present a more comprehensive view of my subject than either the space allowed or the more casual publication demanded.

[Pg vi]

I have to thank the editors of the *Outlook* for the generous hospitality of their columns, and for full freedom to republish what belongs to them.

HORACE PLUNKETT.

The Plunkett House, Dublin,
     April, 1910.

[Pg vii]

TABLE OF CONTENTS

CHAPTER I

The Subject and the Point of View

The subject defined — A reconstruction of rural life in English-speaking communities essential to the progress of Western civilisation — A movement for a new rural civilisation to be proposed — The author's point of view derived from thirty years of Irish and American experience — The physical contrast and moral resemblances in the Irish and American rural problems — Mr. Roosevelt's interest in this aspect of the question — His Conservation and Country Life policies

CHAPTER II

The Launching of Two Roosevelt Policies

The sane emotionalism of American public opinion—Gifford Pinchot as the Apostle of Conservation—His test of national efficiency—Mr. James J. Hill's notable pronouncements upon the wastage of natural resources—The evolution of the Conservation policy—Historical and present causes of national extravagance—The Conference of Governors and their pronouncement [Pg viii] upon Conservation—Mr. Roosevelt's Country Life policy—His estimate of the lasting importance of the Conservation and Country Life ideas—The popularity of the Conservation policy and the lack of interest in the Country Life policy—The Country Life Commission's inquiries and the reality of the problem—The need and opportunity for reconstruction of rural life

CHAPTER III

The Origin and Consequences of Rural Neglect

The origin of rural neglect in English-speaking countries traced to the Industrial Revolution in England—Effect of modern economic changes upon the mutual relations of town and country populations—Respects in which the old relations ought to be restored—Three economic reasons for the study of rural conditions—The social consequences of rural neglect—The political importance of rustic experience to reënforce urban intelligence in modern democracies—The analogue of the European exodus in the United States—The moral aspects of rural neglect—The danger to national efficiency of sacrificing agricultural to commercial and industrial interests—The happy circumstance of Mr. Roosevelt's interest in rural well-being

CHAPTER IV

The Inner Life of the American Farmer

Reasons why the rural problem resulting from [Pg ix] urban predominance exists only in English-speaking countries—Neglect of farmer more easily excused in the United States than elsewhere owing to his apparent prosperity—Country Life Commission's pronouncement on rural backwardness—Why the matter must be taken up by the towns—A survey of American rural life—The problem economically and sociologically considered in the Middle West—Causes and character of rural backwardness in the Southern States—The boll-weevil and the hookworm as illustrations of unconcern for the well-being of rural communities—The problem in the New England States not typically American—The progressive attitude of some communities in the Far West in rural reform

CHAPTER V

The Weak Spot in American Rural Economy

The three elements of a rural existence—Mr. Roosevelt's formula: "Better farming, better business, better living"—A comparative analysis of urban and rural business methods shows that herein lies chief cause of rural backwardness—Reasons why farmers fail to adopt methods of combination—A description of the coöperative system in its application to agriculture—The introduction and development of agricultural coöperation in Ireland—The Raiffeisen Credit Association successful in poorest Irish districts—Summary of coöperative achievement by Irish farmers—British imitation of [Pg x] Irish agricultural organising methods—A criticism of American farmers' organisations—Lack of combination for business purposes the cause of political impotence—Urgent need for a reorganisation of American agriculture upon coöperative lines

CHAPTER VI

The Way to Better Farming and Better Living

The retarded application of science to agriculture and neglect of agricultural education—Present progress in agricultural education—Full benefit of education must await coöperative organisation—Connection between coöperation and social progress—Mr. Roosevelt on the cause and cure of rural discontent—Two views upon the principles of rural betterment—The part coöperation is playing in Irish rural society—General observations on town and country pleasures—The social necessity for a redirection of rural education—The rural labour problem—The position of women in farm life—The reason why the remedy for rural backwardness must come from without—The paradox of the problem

CHAPTER VII

The Two Things Needful

Summary of diagnosis and indication of treatment — Chief aim the coördination of agencies available [Pg xi] for social work in the country — Numerical strength and fine social spirit abroad, but leadership needed — Mutual interest of advocates of Conservation and of rural reform — The psychological difficulty due to predominance of urban idea — Roman history repeating itself in New York — The natural leaders of the Country Life movement to be found in the cities — The objects of the movement defined — Two new institutions to be created; the one executive and organising, the other academic — The National Conservation Association qualified to initiate and direct the movement — Possibly an American Agricultural Organisation Society should be founded for the work — The chief practical work the introduction of agricultural coöperation — Necessity for joining forces with existing philanthropic agencies — Suggested enlistment of country clergy in coöperative propagandism — The Country Life Institute, its purpose and functions — Reason why one body cannot undertake work assigned to the two new institutions — The financial requirements of the Institute — Summary and conclusions

[Pg 3]

THE RURAL LIFE PROBLEM

CHAPTER I

THE SUBJECT AND THE POINT OF VIEW

I submit in the following pages a proposition and a proposal—a distinction which an old-country writer of English may, perhaps, be permitted to preserve. The proposition is that, in the United States, as in other English-speaking communities, the city has been developed to the neglect of the country. I shall not have to labour the argument, as nobody seriously disputes the contention; but I shall trace the main causes of the neglect, and indicate what, in my view, must be its inevitable consequences. If I make my case, it will appear that our civilisation has thus become dangerously one-sided, and that, in the interests of national well-being, [Pg 4] it is high time for steps to be taken to counteract the townward tendency.

My definite proposal to those who accept these conclusions is that a Country Life movement, upon lines which will be laid down, should be initiated by existing associations, whose efforts should be supplemented by a new organisation which I shall call a Country Life Institute. There are in the United States a multiplicity of agencies, both public and voluntary, available for this work. But the army of workers in this field of social service needs two things: first, some definite plan for coördinating their several activities, and, next, some recognised source of information collected from the experience of the Old and the New World. It is the purpose of these pages to show that these needs are real and can be met.

Two obvious questions will here suggest themselves. Why should the United States—of all countries in the world—be chosen for such a theme instead of a country like [Pg 5] Ireland, where the population depends mainly upon agriculture? What qualifications has an Irishman, be he never so competent to advise upon the social and economic problems of his own country, to talk to Americans about the life of their rural population? I admit at once that, while I have made some study of American agriculture and rural economy, my actual work upon the problem of which I write has been restricted to Ireland. But I claim, with some pride, that, in thought upon rural economy, Ireland is ahead of any English-speaking country. She has troubles of her own, some inherent in the adverse physical conditions, and others due to well-known historical causes, that too often impede the action to which her best thoughts should lead. But the very fact that those who grapple with Irish problems have to work through failure to success will certainly not lessen the value to the social student of the experience gained. I recognise, however, that I must give the reader so much of [Pg 6] personal narrative as is required to enable him to estimate the value of my facts, and of the conclusions which I base upon them.

To have enjoyed an Irish-American existence, to have been profoundly interested in, and more or less in touch with, public affairs in both countries, to have been an unwilling politician in Ireland and not a politician at all in America, is, to say the least, an unusual experience for an Irishman. But such has been my record during the last twenty years. Soon after graduating at Oxford, I was advised to live in mountain air for a while, and for the next decade I was a ranchman along the foothills of the Rockies. To those who knew that my heart was in Ireland, I used to explain that I might some day be in politics at home, and must take care of my lungs. In 1889 I returned to live and work in my own country, but I retained business interests, including some farming operations, in the Western States. Ever since then I have taken my annual [Pg 7] holiday across the Atlantic, and have studied rural conditions over a wider area in the United States than my business interests demanded.

For eight years, commencing in 1892, I was a Member of Parliament. My legislative ambition was to get something done for Irish industry, and especially Irish agriculture. Having secured the assistance of an unprecedented combination of representative Irishmen, known as the Recess Committee (because it sat during the Parliamentary recess), we succeeded in getting the addition we wanted to the machinery of Irish Government. The functions of the new institution are sufficiently indicated by its cumbrous Parliamentary title, "The Department of Agriculture and other Industries and for Technical Instruction for Ireland." I mention this official experience because it not only intensified my desire to study American conditions, but it also brought me frequently to Washington to [Pg 8] study the working of those Federal institutions which are concerned for the welfare of the rural population. There I enjoyed the unfailing courtesy of American public servants to the foreign inquirer.

On one of these visits, in the winter of 1905-1906, I called upon President Roosevelt to pay him my respects, and to express to him my obligations to some members of his Administration. I wished especially to acknowledge my indebtedness to that veteran statesman, Secretary Wilson, the value of whose long service to the American farmer it would be hard to exaggerate. Mr. Roosevelt questioned me as to the exact object of my inquiries, and asked me to come again and discuss with him more fully than was possible at the moment certain economic and social questions which had engaged much of his own thoughts. He was greatly interested to learn that in Ireland we have been approaching many of these questions from his own point of view. He made me [Pg 9] tell him the story of Irish land legislation, and of recent Irish movements for the improvement of agricultural conditions. Ever since, his interest in these Irish questions — to *the* Irish Question we gave a wide berth — has been maintained on account of their bearing upon his Rural Life policy, for I had shown him how the economic strengthening and social elevation of the Irish farmer had become a matter of urgent Irish concern. I recall many things he said on that occasion, which show that his two great policies of Conservation and Country Life reform were maturing in his mind. I need hardly say how deeply interesting these policies are to me, embracing as they do economic and social problems, the working out of which in my own country happens to be the task to which I have devoted the best years of my life.

I must now offer to the reader so much of the story of the Country Life movement in my own country as will enable him to [Pg 10] understand its interest to Mr. Roosevelt and to many another worker upon the analogous problems of the United States. Ireland is passing through an agrarian revolution. There, as in many other European countries, the title to most of the agricultural land rested upon conquest. The English attempt to colonise Ireland never completely succeeded nor completely failed; consequently the Irish never ceased to repudiate the title of the alien landlord. In 1881 Mr.

Gladstone introduced one of the greatest agrarian reforms in history — rent-fixing by judicial authority — which was certainly a bold attempt to put an end to a desolating conflict, centuries old.

The scheme failed, — whether, as some hold, from its inherent defects, or from the circumstances of the time, is an open question. It is but fair to its author to point out that a rapidly increasing foreign competition, chiefly from the newly opened tracts of virgin soil in the New World, led to a fall [Pg 11] in agricultural prices, which made the first rents fixed appear too high. Quicker and cheaper transit, together with processes for keeping produce fresh over the longest routes, soon showed that the new market conditions had come to stay. A bad land system on a rising market might succeed better than a good one on a falling. The land tenure reforms begun in 1881, having broken down under stress of foreign competition, and Purchase Acts on a smaller scale having been tentatively tried in the interval, in 1903 Parliament finally decreed that sufficient money should be provided to buy out all the remaining agricultural land. In a not remote future, some two hundred million pounds sterling — a billion dollars — will have been advanced by the British Government to enable the tenants to purchase their holdings, the money to be repaid in easy instalments during periods averaging over sixty years.

Twenty years ago this general course of events was foreseen, and a few Irishmen [Pg 12] conceived and set to work upon what has come to be Ireland's Rural Life policy. The position taken up was simple. What Parliament was about to do would pull down the whole structure of Ireland's agricultural economy, and would clear away the chief hindrance to economic and social progress. But upon the ground thus cleared the edifice of a new rural social economy would have to be built. This work, although it needs the fostering care of government, and liberal facilities for a system of education intimately related to the people's working lives, belongs mainly to the sphere of voluntary effort.

The new movement, which was started in 1889 to meet the circumstances I have indicated, was thus a movement for the up-building of country life. It anticipated the lines of the formula which Mr. Roosevelt adopted in his Message transmitting to Congress the

Report of the Country Life Commission—better farming, better business, [Pg 13] better living: we began with better business, which consisted in the introduction of agricultural coöperation into the farming industry, for several reasons which will appear later, and for one which I must mention here. We found that we could not develop in unorganised farmers a political influence strong enough to enable them to get the Government to do its part towards better farming. Owing to the new agricultural opinion which had been developed indirectly by organising the farmer, we were able to win from Parliament the department I have named above. This institution was so framed and endowed that it is able to give to the Irish farmers all the assistance which can be legitimately given by public agencies and at public expense. The assistance consists chiefly of education. But education is interpreted in the widest sense. Practical instruction to old and young, in schools, upon the farms, and at meetings, lectures, experiments, and demonstrations, the circulation of useful [Pg 14] information and advice, and all the usual methods known to progressive governments, are being introduced with the chief aim of enabling the farmer to apply to the practice of farming the teachings of modern science. Better living, which includes making country life more interesting and attractive, is sought by using voluntary associations, some organised primarily for business purposes, and others, having no business aim, for social and intellectual ends. But Irish rural reformers are agreed that by far the most important step towards a higher and a better rural life would be a redirection of education in the country schools. To this I shall return in the proper place.

I can now proceed with my American experiences without leaving any doubt as to the point of view from which I approach the problem of rural life in the United States. Having engaged in actual work upon that problem in Ireland, where a combination of economic changes and political events has [Pg 15] made its solution imperative, and having been long in personal touch with rural conditions in some Western States, my interest in certain policies which were maturing at Washington may be easily surmised. There I found that, with wholly different conditions to be dealt with, the thoughts of the President and of others in his confidence were, as regards the main issue, moving in the same direction as my own.

They too had come to feel that the welfare of the rural population had been too long neglected, and that it was high time to consider how the neglect might be repaired. In his annual message to Congress in 1904, Mr. Roosevelt had made it clear that he was fully conscious of this necessity. "Nearly half of the people of this country," he wrote, "devote their energies to growing things from the soil. Until a recent date little has been done to prepare these millions for their life work." I did not realise at the time the full import of these sentences. Nor did I foresee that [Pg 16] the problem of rural life was to be forced to the front by the awakening of public opinion, upon another issue differing from and yet closely related to the subject of these pages. Mr. Roosevelt was thinking out the Conservation idea, which I believe will some day be recognised as the greatest of his policies.

[Pg 19]

CHAPTER II

THE LAUNCHING OF TWO ROOSEVELT POLICIES

Although somebody has already said something like it, I would say there is a tide in the thoughts of men which, taken at the flood, leads on to action. We make the general claim for our Western civilisation, that, whatever the form of government, once public opinion is thoroughly stirred upon a great and vital issue, it is but a question of time for the will to find the way. But in the life of the United States, the passage from thought to action is more rapid than in any country that I know. Nowhere do we find such a combination of emotionalism with sanity. No better illustration of these national qualities could be desired than that afforded by the inception and early growth of the Conservation policy.

[Pg 20]

I have already shown how my inquiries at Washington gave me access to the most accessible of the world's statesmen. At the same time there came into my life another remarkable personality. To the

United States Forester of that day I owe my earliest interest in the Conservation policy. In counsel with him I came to regard the Conservation and Rural Life policies as one organic whole. So I must say here a word about the man who, more than any other, has inspired whatever in these pages may be worth printing.

I first met Gifford Pinchot in his office in Washington in 1905. I was not especially interested in forestry, but the Forester was so interesting that I listened with increasing delight to the story of his work. I noticed that as an administrator he had a grasp of detail and a mastery of method which are not usually found in men who have had no training in large business affairs. I thought the secret of his success lay between love [Pg 21] of work and sympathy with workers, which gained him the devotion and enthusiastic coöperation of his staff. It is, however, as a statesman rather than as an administrator that his achievement is and will be known.

When I first knew the Forester, I found that already the conservation of timber was but a small part of his material aims: every national resource must be husbanded. But over the whole scheme of Conservation a great moral issue reigned supreme. He clung affectionately to his task, but it was not to him mere forestry administration. In his far vision he seemed to see men as trees walking. The saving of one great asset was broadening out into insistence upon a new test of national efficiency: the people of the United States were to be judged by the manner in which they applied their physical and mental energies to the conservation and development of their country's natural resources. The acceptance of this test would mean the success of a great policy [Pg 22] for the initiation of which President Roosevelt gave almost the whole credit to Gifford Pinchot.

There is one other name which will be ever honorably associated with the dawn of the Conservation idea which Mr. Roosevelt elevated to the status and dignity of a national policy. In September, 1906, Mr. James J. Hill delivered (under the title of "The Future of the United States") what I think was an epoch-making address. It is significant that this great railway president opened his campaign for the economic salvation of the United States by addressing himself, not to politicians or professors, but to a representative body of Minnesota farmers. This address presented for the first time in popular form a remarkable collection of economic facts, which formed the basis of conclusions as startling as they were new. Let me attempt a brief summary of its contents.

The natural resources, to which the [Pg 23] Conservation policy relates, may be divided into two classes: the minerals, which when used cannot be replaced, and things that grow from the soil, which admit of indefinitely augmented reproduction. At the head of the former category stands the supply of coal and iron. This factor in the nation's industry and commerce was being exhausted at a rate which made it certain that, long before the end of the century, the most important manufactures would be handicapped by a higher cost of production. The supply of merchantable timber was disappearing even more rapidly. But far more serious than all other forms of wastage was the reckless destruction of the natural fertility of the soil. The final result, according to Mr. Hill, must be that within a comparatively brief period—a period for which the present generation was bound to take thought—this veritable Land of Promise would be hard pressed to feed its own people, while the manufactured exports to pay for [Pg 24] imported food would not be forthcoming. It should be added that this sensational forecast was no purposeless jeremiad. Mr. Hill told his hearers that the danger which threatened the future of the Nation would be averted only by the intelligence and industry of those who cultivated the farm lands, and that they had it in their power to provide a perfectly practicable and adequate remedy. This was to be found—if such a condensation be permissible—in the application of the physical sciences to the practice, and of economic science to the business, of farming.

In spite of the immense burden of great undertakings which he carried, Mr. Hill repeated the substance of this address on many occasions. Lord Rosebery once said that speeches were the most ephemeral of all ephemeral things, and for some time it looked as if one of the most important speeches ever delivered by a public man on a great public issue was going to illustrate the truth [Pg 25] of this saying. It seems strange that his facts and arguments should have remained unchallenged, and yet unsupported, by other public men. Perhaps the best explanation is to be found in a recent dictum of Mr. James Bryce. Speaking at the University of California, the

British Ambassador said: "We can all think of the present, and are only too apt to think chiefly about the present. The average man, be he educated or uneducated, seldom thinks of anything else." There are, however, special circumstances in the history of the United States which account for the extraordinary unconcern about what is going to happen to the race in a period which may seem long to those whose personal interest fixes a limit to their gaze, but which is indeed short in the life of a nation. After the religious, political, and military struggles through which the American nation was brought to birth, there followed a century of no less strenuous wrestling with the forces of nature. [Pg 26] That century stands divided by the greatest civil conflict in the world's history; but this only served to strengthen in a united people those indomitable qualities to which the nation owes its leadership in the advancement of civilisation. The abundance (until now considered as virtual inexhaustibility) of natural resources, the call for capital and men for their development, the rich reward of conquest in the field of industry, may explain, but can hardly excuse, a National attitude which seems to go against the strongest human instinct—one not altogether wanting in lower animal life—that of the preservation of the race. It is an attitude which recalls the question said to have been asked by an Irishman: "What has posterity done for me?" But this was before Conservation was in the air.

I have now told what I came by chance to know about the origin of the Conservation idea. The story of its early growth was no less remarkable than the suddenness of its [Pg 27] appearance. In the spring of 1908 matters had advanced so far that the governors of all the States and Territories met to discuss it. Before the Conference broke up they were moved to "declare the conviction that the great prosperity of our country rests upon the abundant resources of the land chosen by our forefathers for their homes," that these resources are "a heritage to be made use of in establishing and promoting the comfort, prosperity, and happiness of the American people, but not to be wasted, deteriorated, or needlessly destroyed; that this material basis is threatened with exhaustion"; that "conservation of our natural resources is a subject of transcendent importance which should engage unremittingly the attention of the Nation, the States, and the people in earnest coöperation"; and that "this coöperation should find expression in suitable action by the Congress and by the legislatures of the several States."

It is, of course, not with Conservation, but [Pg 28] with Rural Life, that we are here directly concerned; but it should be borne in mind that the chief of all the nation's resources is the fertility of the soil. More than one competent authority declared at the Conference of Governors that this national asset was the subject of the greatest actual waste, and was at the same time capable of the greatest development and conservation. This interdependence of the two Roosevelt policies—the fact that neither of them can come to fruition without the success of the other—makes those of us who work for rural progress rest our chief hopes upon the newly aroused public opinion in the American Republic.

To my knowledge this view is shared by President Roosevelt, who always regarded his Conservation and Rural Life policies as complementary to each other. The last time I saw him—it was on Christmas Eve, 1908—he dwelt on this aspect of his public work and aims. I remember how he [Pg 29] expressed the hope that, when the more striking incidents of his Administration were forgotten, public opinion would look kindly upon his Conservation and Rural Life policies. I ventured upon the confident prediction that he would not be disappointed in this anticipation. Already the authors of the Conservation policy have been rewarded by a general acceptance of the principle for which they stand. The national conscience now demands that the present generation, while enjoying the material blessings with which not only nature but also the labour and sacrifices of their forefathers have so bounteously endowed them, shall have due regard for the welfare of those who are to come after them.

Americans, who are accustomed to rapid developments in public opinion, will hardly appreciate the impression made by the story I have just told upon the mind of an observer from old countries, where action does not tread upon the heels of thought. But surely [Pg 30] an amazing thing has happened. In the life of one Administration a great idea seizes the mind of the American people. This leads to a stock-taking of natural resources and a searching of the national conscience. Then, suddenly, there emerges a quite new national policy. Conceived during the last Administration, when it brought Mr. Roosevelt and Mr. Bryan on to the same platform, Conservation at once rose above party, and will be the accepted policy of all future Administrations. It has already secured almost Pan-American endorsement at its birthplace in Washington. The fathers of Conservation are now looking forward to a still larger sphere of influence for their offspring at an International Conference which it is hoped to assemble at the Hague.

But it must be admitted that no such reception was accorded to Mr. Roosevelt's other policy, to which our attention must now be turned. The reasons for the comparative lack of interest in the problem of [Pg 31] Rural Life are many and complex, but two of them may be noted in passing. Conservation calls for legislative and administrative action, and this always sets up a ferment in the political mind. The Rural Life idea, on the other hand, though it will demand some governmental assistance, must rely mainly upon voluntary effort. The methods necessary for its development, and their probable results, are also less obvious, and thus less easily appreciated by the public. Whatever the reason, while Conservation has rushed into the forefront of public interest and has won the status and dignity of a policy, the sister idea is still struggling for a platform, and its advocates must be content to see their efforts towards a higher and a better country life regarded as a movement.

This estimate of the relative positions of these two ideas in the public mind will, I think, be borne out when we contrast the quiet initiation of the movement with the dramatic début of the policy. For all the [Pg 32] officialism with which it was launched, President Roosevelt's Country Life Commission might as well have been appointed by some wealthy philanthropist who would, at least, have paid its members' travelling expenses, [1] and private initiation might also have spared us the ridicule which greeted the alleged proposal to "uplift" a body of citizens who were told that they were already adorning the heights of American civilisation. The names of the men who volunteered for this unpaid service should have been a sufficient guarantee that theirs was no fool's errand. [2]

[Pg 33]

How real was the problem the commissioners were investigating was abundantly proved to those who were present when they got into touch with working farmers and their wives, and discussed freely and informally the conditions, human and material, to which the problem of Rural Life relates. I shall refer again to their report. But I may here say I am firmly convinced that a complete change in the whole attitude of public opinion towards the old question of town and country must precede any large practical outcome to the labours of the Commission. It has to be brought home to those who lead public opinion that for many decades we, the English-speaking peoples, have been unconsciously guilty of having gravely neglected one side, and that perhaps the most important side, of Western civilisation.

To sustain this judgment I must now view the sequence of events which led to the subordination of rural to urban interests, and try to estimate its probable consequences. It [Pg 34] will be seen that the neglect is comparatively recent, and of English origin. I believe that the New World offers just now a rare opportunity for launching a movement which will be directed to a reconstruction of rural life. It is this belief which has prompted an Irish advocate of rural reform to turn his thoughts away for a brief space from the poorer peasantry of his own country and to take counsel with his fellow-workers in the United States and Canada on a problem which affects them all.

FOOTNOTES:

[1] These, as a matter of fact, were defrayed by the trustees of the Russell Sage Foundation.

[2] The Commission consisted of L. H. Bailey, of the New York State College of Agriculture at Cornell University (chairman); Henry Wallace, editor of *Wallace's Farmer*, Des Moines, Iowa; Kenyon L. Butterfield, President of the Massachusetts Agricultural College, Amherst, Massachusetts; Walter H. Page, editor of *The World's Work*, New York City; Gifford Pinchot, United States Forester, and Chairman of the National Conservation Commission; C. S. Barrett, President of the Farmers' Co-operative and Educational Union of America, Union City, Georgia; W. A. Beard, of the *Great West Magazine*, Sacramento, California.

[Pg 37]

CHAPTER III

THE ORIGIN AND CONSEQUENCES OF RURAL NEGLECT

The most radical economic change which history records set in during the last half of the eighteenth century in England, as the result of that remarkable achievement of modern civilisation, the Industrial Revolution. Mechanical inventions changed all industry, setting up the factories of the town instead of the scattered home production of the country and its villages. In the wake of the new inventions economic science stepped in, and, scrupulously obeying its own law of demand and supply, told the then predominant middle classes just what they wished to be told. Adam Smith had made the wonderful discovery that money and wealth were not the same thing. Then [Pg 38] Ricardo, and after him the Manchester School of economists, made division of labour the cardinal virtue in the new gospel of wealth. In order to give full play to this economic principle all workers in mechanical industries were huddled together in the towns. There they were to be transformed from capricious, undisciplined humans into mechanical attachments, and restricted to such functions as steam-driven automata had not yet learned to perform. That was the first stage of the Industrial Revolution, with its chief consequences, the rural exodus and urban overcrowding. It is a hideous nightmare to look back upon from these more enlightened days. Well might the angels weep over the flight of all that was best from the God-made country to the man-made town.

Before the middle of the last century the clouds began to lift. For a while the good Lord Shaftesbury seemed to be crying in the wilderness of middle-class plutocracy, but it [Pg 39] was not long before the crying of the children in their factories stirred the national conscience. The health of nations was allowed to be considered as well as their wealth. Social and political science rose up in protest against both the economists and the manufacturers. There followed a period of beneficent social changes, no less radical than those which the new mechanical inventions had produced in the economics of industry. The factory town of to-day presents a strange contrast to that which sacrificed humanity to material aggrandisement. What with its shortened hours of labour, superior artisan dwellings, improved sanitation, parks, open spaces and playgrounds, free instruction and cheap entertainment for old and young, hospitals and charities, rapid transportation, a popular Press, and full political freedom, the modern hive of industry stands as a monument of what, under liberal laws, can be done by education and organisation to realise the higher aspirations of a people.

[Pg 40]

During this second period, another economic development produced upon the attitude of the urban mind towards the rural population an effect to which, I think, has not been given the consideration it deserves. Better and cheaper transportation, with the consequent establishment of what the economists call the world-market, completely changed the relationship between the townsman and the farmer. A sketch of their former mutual relations will make my meaning clear. Within the last century every town relied largely for its food supply on the produce of the fields around its walls. The countrymen coming into the weekly market were the chief customers for the wares of the town craftsmen. In this primitive state of trade, townsmen could not but realise the importance to themselves of a prosperous country population around them. But this simple exchange, as we all know, has developed into the complex commercial operations of modern times. [Pg 41] To-day most large towns derive their household stuff from the food-growing tracts of the whole world, and I doubt whether any are dependent on the neighbouring farmers, or feel themselves specially concerned for their welfare. I do not think the general truth of this picture will be questioned, and I hope some consideration may be given to the conclusions I now draw.

In the transition we are considering, the reciprocity between the producers of food and the raw material of clothes on the one hand, and manufacturers and general traders of the towns on the other, has not ceased; it has actually increased since the days of steam and electricity. But it has become national, and even international, rather than local. Town consumers are still dependent upon agricultural producers, who, in turn, are much larger consumers than formerly of all kinds of commodities made in towns. Forty-two per cent of materials used in manufacture in the United States are from the farm, [Pg 42] which also contributes seventy per cent of the country's exports. But in the complexity of these trade developments townsmen have been cut off more and more from personal contact with the country, and in this way have lost their sense of its importance. My point is that the shifting of the trade relationship of town and country from its former local to its present national and international basis in reality increases their interdependence. And I hold most strongly that until in this matter the obligations of a common citizenship are realised by the town, we cannot hope for any lasting National progress.

Whatever be the causes which have begotten the neglect of rural life, no one will gainsay the wisdom of estimating the consequences. These are economic, social, and political; and I will discuss them briefly under these heads. There are three main economic reasons which suggest a closer study of rural conditions. First, there is the interdependence of town and country, less obvious [Pg 43] than it was in the days of the local market, but no less real. Any fall in the number, or decline in the efficiency, of the farming community, will be accompanied by a corresponding fall in the country sale of town products. This is especially true of America, where the foreign commerce is unimportant in comparison with internal trade. To nourish country life is the best way to help home trade. And quite as important as these considerations is the effect which good or bad farming must have upon the cost of living to the whole population. Excessive middle profits between producer and consumer may largely account for the very serious rise in the price of staple articles of food. This is a fact of the utmost significance, but, as I shall show later, the remedy for too high a cost of production and distribution lies with the farmer, the improvement of whose business methods will be seen to be the chief factor in the reform which the Rural Life movement must attempt to introduce.

[Pg 44]

The essential dependence of nations on agriculture is the second economic consideration. The author of "The Return to the Land," Senator Jules Méline (successively Minister of Agriculture, Minister of Commerce and Premier of France), tells us that this remarkable book is "merely an expansion of a profound thought uttered long ago by a Chinese philosopher: 'The well-being of a people is like a tree; agriculture is its root, manufacture and commerce are its branches and its life; if the root is injured the leaves fall, the branches break away and the tree dies.'"

This truth is not hard to apply to the conditions of to-day. The income of every country depends on its natural resources, and on the skill and energy of its inhabitants; and the quickest way to increase the income is to concentrate on the production of those articles for which there is the greatest demand throughout the commercial world. The relentless application of this principle has been [Pg 45] characteristic of the nineteenth century. But the augmentation of income has in one special way been purchased by a diminution of capital. The industrial movement has been based on an immense expenditure of coal and iron; and in America and Great Britain the coal and iron which can be cheaply obtained are within measurable distance of exhaustion. As these supplies diminish, the industrial leadership of America and Great Britain must disappear, unless they can employ their activities in other forms of industry. Those, therefore, who desire that the English-speaking countries should maintain for many ages that high position which they now occupy, should do all in their power to encourage a proper system of agriculture—the one industry in which the fullest use can be made of natural resources without diminishing the inheritance of future generations—the industry "about which," Mr. James J. Hill emphatically declares, "all others revolve, and by which future America shall stand or fall."

[Pg 46]

The third economic reason will hardly be disputed. Agricultural prosperity is an important factor in financial stability. The fluctuations of commerce depend largely on the good and bad harvests of the world, but, as they do not coincide with them in time, their violence is, on the whole, likely to be less in a nation where agricultural and manufacturing interests balance each other, than in one depending mainly or entirely on either. The small savings of numerous farmers, amounting in the aggregate to very large sums, are a powerful means of steadying the money market; they are not liable to the vicissitudes nor attracted by the temptations which affect the larger investors. They remain a permanent national resource, which, as the experience of France proves, may be confidently drawn upon in time of need. I have often thought that, were it not for the thrift and industry of the French peasantry, financial crises would be as frequent in France as political upheavals.

[Pg 47]

As regards the social aspect of rural neglect, I suggest that the city may be more seriously concerned than is generally imagined for the well-being of the country. One cannot but admire the civic pride with which Americans contemplate their great centres of industry and commerce, where, owing to the many and varied improvements, the townsman of the future is expected to unite the physical health and longevity of the Bœotian with the mental superiority of the Athenian. But we may ask whether this somewhat optimistic forecast does not ignore one important question. Has it been sufficiently considered how far the moral and physical health of the modern city depends upon the constant influx of fresh blood from the country, which has ever been the source from which the town draws its best citizenship? You cannot keep on indefinitely skimming the pan and have equally good milk left. In America the drain may continue a while longer without the inevitable consequences [Pg 48] becoming plainly visible. But sooner or later, if the balance of trade in this human traffic be not adjusted, the raw material out of which urban society is made will be seriously deteriorated, and the symptoms of National degeneracy will be properly charged against those who neglected to foresee the evil and treat the cause. It is enough for my present purpose if it be admitted that the people of every state are largely bred in rural districts, and that the physical and moral well-being of these districts must eventually influence the quality of the whole people.

I come now to the political considerations which, I think, have not been sufficiently taken into account. In most countries political life depends largely for its steadiness and sanity upon a strong infusion of rural opinion into the counsels of the nation. It is a truism that democracy requires for success a higher level of intelligence and character in the mass of the people than other forms [Pg 49] of government. But intelligence alone is not enough for the citizen of a democracy; he must have experience as well, and the experience of a townsman is essentially imperfect. He has generally a wider theoretical knowledge than the rustic of the main processes by which the community lives; but the rustic's practical knowledge of the more fundamental of them is wider than the townsman's. He knows actually and in detail how corn is grown and how beasts are bred, whereas the town artisan hardly knows how the whole of any one article of commerce is made. The townsman sees and takes part in the wonderful achievements of industrial science without any full understanding of its methods or of the relative importance and the interaction of the forces engaged. To this one-sided experience may be attributed in some measure that disregard of inconvenient facts, and that impatience of the limits of practicability, which many observers note as a characteristic defect of popular government.

[Pg 50]

However that may be, there is one symptom in modern politics of which the gravity is generally acknowledged, while its special connection with the towns is an easily ascertainable fact; I mean the

40

growth of the cruder forms of Socialism. The town artisan or labourer, who sees displayed before him vast masses of property in which he has no share, and contrasts the smallness of his remuneration with the immense results of his labour, is easily attracted to remedies worse than the disease. A fuller and more exact understanding of the means by which the wealth of the community is created is, for the townsman, the best antidote to mischievous agitation so far as it is not merely the result of poverty. But the countryman, especially the proprietor of a piece of land, however small, is protected from this infection. The atmosphere in which Socialism of the predatory kind can grow up does not exist among a prosperous farming community—perhaps because in the country [Pg 51] the question of the divorce of the worker from his raw material by capitalism does not arise. The farm furnishes the raw material of the farmer; yet he cannot be said to spend his life creating the alleged "surplus value" of Marxian doctrine. For these reasons I suggest that the orderly and safe progress of democracy demands a strong agricultural population. It is as true now as when Aristotle said it that "where husbandmen and men of small fortune predominate government will be guided by law."

I have now shown that for every reason the interests of the rural population ought no longer to be subordinated to those of the city. That such has been the tendency in English-speaking countries will hardly be questioned. In Great Britain the rural exodus has gone on with a vengeance. The last census (1901) showed that seventy-seven per cent of the population was urban, and only twenty-three per cent rural. A few years ago there were derelict farms within easy walk of [Pg 52] the outskirts of London. In Ireland the rural exodus took the form of emigration, mainly to American cities, and this has been the chief factor in the reduction of the population in sixty years from more than eight millions to a trifle above four. But it may be thought that in the United States no similar tendency is in operation. Certainly those who admit the townward drift of country life may fairly say that it does not present so urgent a problem in the New World as in parts of the Old. Even granting that this is so, the fact remains that the town population of America is seriously outgrowing the rural population; for, while the towns are growing hugely, the country stands still. Moreover, we must not forget that,

Australia apart, America is even still the most underpopulated part of the globe. We are accustomed to think Ireland underpopulated, owing to emigration, yet even to-day the scale of population is almost six times greater than that of the United States. If the Union [Pg 53] were peopled as thickly as Ireland even still is, the population would be nearly five hundred millions. There is still a vast deal of filling-up to be done in America, mostly in the rural parts.

But the main consideration I wish to emphasise throughout is that the problem under review is moral and social far more than economic, human rather than material. This is the natural view of an Irish worker, who knows that the solution of *his* problem depends upon the possibility of endowing country life with such social improvements as will provide an effective compensation for a necessarily modest standard of comfort. But the citizens of the United States may be pardoned for being physiocrats. The statistical proof, annually furnished, of the growing agricultural wealth, is apt to obscure other essentials of progress. The astronomical proportions of the figures stagger the imagination, and engender the kind of pride a man feels when he is first [Pg 54] told the number of red corpuscles luxuriating in his blood. How can there be agricultural depression in a country whose farm lands Secretary Wilson, in his notable Annual Report for 1905, declared to have increased in value over a period of five years at the astounding rate of $3,400,000 per day? Yet to the deeper insight, the same moral influence through which we in Ireland are seeking to combat the evils of material poverty may in the United States be needed as a moral corrective to a too rapidly growing material prosperity. The patriotic American, who thinks of the life of the Nation rather than of the individual, will, if he looks beneath the surface, discern in this God-prospered country symptoms of rural decadence fraught with danger to National efficiency.

The reckless sacrifice of agricultural interests by the legislators of the towns is condemned by the verdict of history. We need not now fear that invading hordes of hardy [Pg 55] barbarians will mar the destiny of the great Western Republic, as they ended the career of the Roman Empire. There are, however, other clouds upon the horizon. Only a few years ago, the American people could well treat with contempt the bogy of the Yellow Peril. With a transformation unprecedented in history, the situation has been changed. Japan is already devoting to the arts of peace qualities but yesterday displayed in war, to the amazement of the Western world. In another Eastern empire there are vast resources—especially coal and iron in juxtaposition—awaiting only industrial leadership to utilise a practically limitless labour supply for their development. These are facts worthy of consideration for their potential bearing upon the industrial and commercial standing of the United States.

To the onlooker, it does seem a happy circumstance that there has just been, for seven critical years, at the head of American [Pg 56] affairs the strenuous advocate of the strenuous life. I read through his Messages the warning that in the struggle for preëminence the ultimate victory will lie with those nations who found their prosperity on the high physical and ethical condition of the people. That is the oldest, as it is the latest, wisdom of the East. It is in this spirit that the neglected problem of Rural Life should now be given some share of the attention hitherto devoted to the life of the towns.

[Pg 59]

CHAPTER IV

THE INNER LIFE OF THE AMERICAN FARMER

I recently asked a German economist if he could tell me the best books to read upon the problem of rural life in Germany. His reply was: "There are no books, because there is no problem." It is generally true, no doubt, that the Rural Life problem, in so far as it consists in the subordination of the country to the town, is peculiar to the English-speaking countries, where it seems to be mainly attributable to three causes. The chief of these was no doubt the Industrial Revolution in England, of which enough has already been said. Secondly, in the United States and in some portions of the British Empire, the opening up of vast tracts of virgin soil led not unnaturally to the postponement of social development until the pioneer [Pg 60] farmers had settled down to the new life. The third cause was immunity from the danger of foreign invasion, which eliminated the military reasons for maintaining a numerous, virile, and progressive rural population.

There are many in England who regret that it should have been forgotten how the English owed their commercial supremacy to the fighting qualities of the old yeoman class. In the United States it should be remembered that nowadays peace strength is quite as important as war strength, and it may be questioned whether there can be any sustained industrial efficiency where the great body of workers who conduct the chief—the only absolutely necessary— industry are wasting the resources at their command by bad husbandry. We may, however, concede that the neglect of rural life is much easier to explain and excuse in the United States than in the older English-speaking countries. Quite apart from the abundance of agricultural resources which the American farmers enjoy, [Pg 61] it might well be thought that the rural communities are keeping pace with the progress of urban civilisation. The citizens who now occupy the farm lands of the United States have been largely drawn from the pick of the European peasantries. In the days of their coming, it took courage and enterprise to face the now almost forgotten terrors of the Atlantic Ocean. These immigrants, and the migrants from the Eastern States, have profited enormously by their change of residence. Their material well-being has already been admitted, and, with rare exceptions, they have displayed no overt symptoms of agrarian discontent.

It must not, however, be imagined that the apparent apathy of American farmers is due to contentment. Like others of their calling, they keep a full stock of grievances in their mental stores. They have very definite opinions as to what is wrong, but to these opinions no formal expression is given. They vaguely feel that they would like to remould [Pg 62] "the sorry scheme of things entire," but they lack the public spirit which is required before concerted action can be taken successfully. The Country Life Commission held a series of conferences throughout the United States, which brought them into the closest touch with every type of American farm life. They received written replies from some 125,000 rural folk to whom they had sent a circular with a dozen questions covering the essential heads of inquiry. The Commissioners say in their report: "We have

44

found by the testimony, not only of the farmers themselves, but of all persons in touch with farm life, more or less serious unrest in every part of the United States, even in the most prosperous regions."

The truth is that, while judged by the standard of living of European peasantries, the farmers of the United States are prosperous, in comparison with the other citizens of the most progressive country in the world they are not well-off. Their accumulation [Pg 63] of material wealth is unnaturally and unnecessarily restricted; their social life is barren; their political influence is relatively small. American farmers have been used by politicians, but have still to learn how to use them. This may be due to the fact that my countrymen elected to devote their genius for organisation to the problems of city government. And in the sphere of private action they are, as will be seen when I discuss the need for a reorganisation of their business, even less effective than in public affairs.

It will be conceded that any hopeful plan to put things right will have to rely upon the organised efforts of those immediately concerned. Both in the sphere of governmental action, and in the vastly more important field of voluntary effort, the moving force will have to be public opinion. But the thought of the farming communities has long ago joined the rural exodus; and before the country life idea can find expression in an effective country life movement, those who [Pg 64] are thinking out the problem will have to commend their arguments to the thought of the towns. Therefore I address these pages, not to farmers only, but to the general reader—who, I may observe, does not generally read if he happens to live in the open country.

In the course of my own studies of American rural life I have found it convenient to divide the United States into four sections, each of them more or less homogeneous. As this method of treatment may help my readers, I will give them a look at my map of American rural life. The four sections may be called the North Eastern, the Middle Western, the Southern, and the Far Western. The division has no pretensions to be scientific; the boundaries can be adjusted to fit in with the experience of each reader.

In my North Eastern section I include the New England States, New York, New Jersey, and most of Pennsylvania. This is a section where manufacturing communities have long [Pg 65] been established, where migration from country to town has been most marked, and where the competition of the newly settled Western farm lands has been followed by effects upon agricultural society very similar to those produced by the same causes in many a rural community on the Continent of Europe. Second comes the Middle Western section, consisting mainly of the Mississippi Valley, with its vast area of high average fertility, the greatest food-producing tract on the continent. Third, I place the Southern section, where the governing factors in rural economy are the climate, the numerical strength of the colored population, the two staple industrial crops — cotton and tobacco — the comparatively recent abolition of slavery, and the long-drawn-out effects of the Civil War. My fourth division, the Far Western section, includes the ranching lands of the arid belt with their irrigation oases, and the fruit-growing and farming lands of the Pacific Coast.

[Pg 66]

As we are discussing the problem chiefly in its human aspect, which affects alike communities wealthy and impoverished, large and small, old-settled and newly established, it will not matter essentially where we first direct our attention for the purpose of illustration. But if, as I hold, nothing less than a reconstruction of rural civilisation is called for, our inquiries will be more profitably directed to those sections where agricultural society is permanently established, or where the rural population might abandon the migratory habit if the conditions were more favorable to an advanced civilisation. At the present stage I feel that the whole subject can be most profitably discussed in its application to the Middle Western and the Southern sections. Here the intimate relationship of the Conservation and the Country Life ideas is best illustrated. Here, too, we get into touch with the problem at its two extremes of prosperity and poverty, each in its own way retarding the progress of rural [Pg 67] civilisation. In both sections the conditions are typical, and distinctively American.

Let us then consider first the general course of rural civilisation in the great food-producing tract of the Middle West. I have in my mind the portion I know best, the last-settled part of the corn belt. Thirty years ago I saw something of the newcomers who settled in this section, where there was still much raw land. These settlers, knowing that the land must rise rapidly in value, almost invariably purchased much larger farms than they could handle. They often sank their available working capital in making the first payments for their land, and went heavily into debt for the balance. They became "land poor," and, in order to meet the instalments of purchase and the high interest on their mortgages, they invented a system of farming unprecedented in its wastefulness. The farm was treated as a mine, or, to use Mr. James J. Hill's metaphor, as a bank where the depositors are always taking out [Pg 68] more than they put in. A corn crop, year after year, without rotation or fertilisers, satisfied the new conception of husbandry—the easiest and least costly extraction of the wealth in the soil. Land, labour, capital, and ability I had been taught to regard as the essentials of production; but here capital was reduced to the minimum, and ability left to nature. Many of the young men who took Horace Greeley's advice and went West knew nothing about farming. I remember writing home that I was in a country where the rolling stone gathered most moss. Possibly the method adopted was the quickest way to get rich; living on capital is all right provided somebody will replace the squandered resources. While there were ample unoccupied lands, Uncle Sam looked kindly upon these enterprising pioneers. It was only in the second Roosevelt Administration that it dawned upon the national conscience that the nation had some claim to be considered as well as the individual. Of course [Pg 69] all this is changed now; although I am not sure that western Canada is not being educated in soil exhaustion by some of these extemporised husbandmen whose habits and temperament lead them to seek "fresh fields and pastures new." "We are not out here for our health," was the reply I got when I showed that my old-fashioned economic sense was shocked by this substitution of land speculation for farming.

I am aware that this very uneconomic procedure is capable of some plausible explanations. The opening up of the vast new territory by the provision of local traffic for transcontinental lines was an object of national urgency and importance. Nevertheless, I think it must now be regretted that a little more thought was not given to the general problem of rural economy, of which transit is but one factor. This may be that irritating kind of wisdom which comes after the event, but I cannot help regarding the policy of rewarding rail-road enterprises [Pg 70] with unconditional grants of vast areas of agricultural land as one of the many evidences of the urban domi-nation over rural affairs.

Of the earlier settled portions of this section I cannot speak from personal knowledge. But a recent magazine article, [3] "The Agrari-an Revolution in the Middle West," follows closely the line of my own thoughts. In this article Mr. Joseph B. Ross, of Lafayette, Indi-ana, who is making a special study of the evolution of American rural life, considers it in three periods: from 1800 to 1835, from 1835 to 1890, and from 1890 to the present time. In the middle period he shows how the most progressive families raised their standard of living steadily with the growing prosperity of the country. They built themselves stately homes with substantial barns. The farmer was developing into a citizen with the solid virtues, the virile inde-pendence, the strong political opinions, religious [Pg 71] interest, and social instincts which characterised the English yeoman of the preceding century. The social life which these communities built up, as soon as their economic position was assured, was a reflection of the best English traditions—it centred round the churches and the Sunday-school. There was a growing distribution of literature as well as organisation for intellectual, educational and social purpos-es. Mr. Ross notes the winter excursions to Florida and California, the adornment of the homes, and many other evidences of a social progress developing a character of its own. During this period there was a migration from the country homes to the cities; but it was only the natural outflow of the surplus members of the rural fami-lies into the professional and business life of the growing centres of commerce and industry.

In the period through which we are now passing a transformation is taking place. The rural exodus is no longer that of [Pg 72] indi-viduals, but of whole families. The farms thus vacated are let to tenants, generally on a three years' lease, at a competition rent. The Country Life Commission says that this tendency to move to the cities "is not peculiar to any region. In difficult farming regions, and where the competition with other farming sections is most severe, the young people may go to town to better their condition. In the best regions the older people retire to town because it is socially more attractive, and they see a prospect of living in comparative ease and comfort on the rental of their lands. Nearly everywhere there is a townward movement for the purpose of securing school advantages for the children. All this tends to sterilize the open country and to lower its social status." The Commission points out that the new addition of what is likely to be a stationary element, whose economic interests lie elsewhere, to the citizenship of the town, may create there a new social problem, while the [Pg 73] tenant in the country will not have that interest in building up rural society which might be expected in the owners of land. Mr. Ross's studies lead him very definitely to the same conclusion. Churches and educational institutions, he tells us, are being starved, and rural society is fast reverting to the type which was prevalent from thirty to fifty years ago. But there is one great difference between then and now. Then, rural civilisation was passing through a stage of marked social advancement which was common throughout the country; now, there are distinct indications of social degeneration, which Mr. Ross regards as the inevitable consequence of the new landlord and tenant system. Many members of these communities must have left the Old World to escape from the selfsame conditions which they are reproducing in the New.

Rural society in the Middle West, as it presents itself to the observer whose authority I have cited, is obviously in a [Pg 74] transitional stage. The lack of farm labourers, which is the common subject of complaint by farmers in all parts of the United States, cannot fail to be aggravated by the change in the conditions of tenancy just noted. The man whose chief concern is to get the most out of the land, at the least expense, in two or three years, will not treat his labourers so well—nor the land so well—as will the man who means to spend his life on the farm; and therefore the labourers will not stay. This scarcity of labour may be met to some extent by an increased use of machinery; but it is more likely to lead to poorer cultivation, which means the depopulation of agricultural districts. England and Ireland furnish too many examples of the rural decay immortalised in Goldsmith's "Deserted Village." It would be strange and sad if the experience were to be repeated on the richest soil of America.

In the Southern section we find a wastefulness similar to that in the corn belt, but due [Pg 75] to wholly different causes. The communities are old-settled, but in many instances they are still abnormally depressed by the terrible effects of the great war, followed by a period of social and economic stagnation. Here there was little but agriculture for the people to rely upon, and their methods have, until recent years, been very backward. The growing of the same crops year after year upon the same fields, the neglect of precaution against the washing away of the soil surface, and the failure to use fertilisers, have made the profits of tillage disappointingly small. Billions of dollars have been lost by these communities through persistent soil exhaustion and erosion. In the last few years the Federal Department of Agriculture has maintained a most efficient staff of agricultural experts under the direction of Dr. Knapp, one of the ablest organisers of farm improvement I have ever met. The General Education Board, who administer large sums provided by Mr. Rockefeller, recognising [Pg 76] the educational value of Dr. Knapp's operations, are contributing about one hundred thousand dollars a year to his work. Dr. Knapp and his field agents have no difficulty at all in demonstrating that the yield may be doubled, and the cost of production greatly reduced, merely by the application of the most elementary science to agriculture. I heard him tell of a farmer whom he had induced to allow his boy — still attending school — to cultivate one acre under his instructions. In the result the boy quadrupled the number of bushels of corn to the acre that his father, following the traditional methods, was able to raise. It would be easy to multiply such instances of thriftlessness and neglected opportunity, of poverty within easy reach of abundance, which have brought it about that the future of the nation is actually endangered by the failure of the food supply to keep pace with the increase of its still relatively sparse population.

The Southern section furnishes two [Pg 77] illustrations of longstanding neglect, both well worthy of consideration for their pregnant suggestiveness. The Federal Department of Agriculture recently scored a notable success in dealing with an insect pest which was threatening the cotton-growing industry with economic ruin. The boll-weevil, like the legal and medical professions, thrives upon the follies of humanity. It attacks the cotton plants which have been weakened by bad husbandry. The scientists did not succeed in finding in the commonwealth of bugs the natural enemy of the pest they were after, but Dr. Knapp, with the wisdom which prefers prevention to cure, seized the opportunity of teaching cotton-growers to diversify their cultivation. The consequence was that the cotton crop itself is gradually responding to the treatment. Many other crops are adding their quota to the produce of the Southern farms, and an all-round improvement, moral as well as material, is accompanying the educational discipline [Pg 78] through which this reformer is putting the communities with whom and for whom he is working.

There is another pest in the South which does not attack the farm crops, but goes straight for the farmer. If the Country Life Commission had done nothing more, they would have justified their appointment by the attention they called to the ravages of the hookworm, which have, no one knows how long, scourged the poor white communities in the Southern States. The effect of the disease set up by the hookworm, which infests the intestines, is a complete sapping of all energy, mental and physical. Mr. Rockefeller has provided a million dollars for the necessary research work and for such subsequent organisation of sanitary effort as may be required to extirpate this unquestionably preventable evil. I wonder how long such a state of affairs would have been permitted to interfere with the health and to paralyse the industry of urban [Pg 79] communities. Had the hookworm, instead of lurking in country lanes, walked the streets, how would it have fared?

These two pests furnish a fine illustration of the length to which the neglect of rural life has been allowed to go in the Southern States.

Neither the Eastern nor the Far Western section presents aspects of special interest to the foreign student of the Rural problem in the United States, but in both the constructive statesman and the social worker will find a rich field for their efforts. In the New England States — more especially in the manufacturing districts — the competition between town and country for labour is as marked as in Industrial England. In this section, however, the lure of the city has a rival in the call of the West, which still makes its appeal to the farmer's boy. Secretary Wilson has recently given it as his opinion that land-seekers who pass by the farms now offered for sale in the western portions [Pg 80] of New York State often go further and fare worse. In these relatively low-priced lands, it ought not to be difficult for agricultural communities to establish permanently a rural society worthy of American ideas of progress. But to do this is to solve the problem we are discussing. We have some other aspects of that problem to consider before we can agree upon the essentials of a philosophic and comprehensive scheme for the rehabilitation of rural life—before we can lay down the lines of a movement to give effect to our plan.

The Far Western section has hardly yet emerged from the frontier-pioneer stage, and its rural problem is still below the horizon. I may, however, note in passing a few evidences that the people of this section have already shown a very real concern for rural progress. The fruit-growers of the Pacific Coast have, in the coöperative marketing of their produce, made an excellent beginning in a matter of first importance in any scheme [Pg 81] of rural development. On irrigation farm lands there has been developed, in connection with the upkeep and control of the water systems, a community spirit which will surely lead to many forms of organisation for mutual economic and social advantage. In the city of Spokane, Washington, the Chamber of Commerce has aroused a public interest in the work of the Country Life Commission which, so far as my information goes, has not been equalled elsewhere in the United States. The Chamber is republishing the Report of the Commission, for which no Federal appropriation appears to have been made. It would seem to be a not wild speculation that the statesmen and social workers who will first solve the rural problem of the English-speaking peoples may be found in the Far West of the New World as well as of the Old.

I must now conclude the diagnosis of rural decadence by a consideration of what in my judgment is the chief cause of the malady, [Pg 82] and so get to a point where we can determine the nature of the remedy. It will then remain only to sketch the outlines of the movement which is to give practical effect to the agreed principles in the life of rural communities.

FOOTNOTE:

[3] *North American Review*, September, 1909.

[Pg 85]

CHAPTER V

THE WEAK SPOT IN AMERICAN RURAL ECONOMY

The evidence of competent American witnesses proves that there is, in the United States, notwithstanding its immense agricultural wealth, a Rural Life problem. Here, as elsewhere, on a fuller analysis, the utmost variety of race, soil, climate and market facilities serve but to emphasise the importance of the human factor. But this consideration does not lessen the need for a sternly practical treatment of the rural social economy under review. In this chapter, I propose to go right down to the roots of the rural problem, find what is wrong with the industry by which the country people live, and see how it can be righted. We should then [Pg 86] have clearly in our minds the essentials of prosperity in a rural community.

Agriculture, the basis of a rural existence, must be regarded as a science, as a business and as a life. I have already adverted to President Roosevelt's formula for solving the rural problem—"better farming, better business, better living." Better farming simply means the application of modern science to the practice of agriculture. Better business is the no less necessary application of modern commercial methods to the business side of the farming industry. Better living is the building up, in rural communities, of a domestic and social life which will withstand the growing attractions of the modern city.

This threefold scheme of reform covers the whole ground and will become the basis of the Country Life movement to be suggested later. But in the working out of the general scheme, there must be one important change in the order of procedure [Pg 87] —'better business' must come first. The dull commercial details of agriculture have been sadly neglected, perhaps on account of the more human interest of the scientific and social aspects of country life. Yet my own experience in working at the rural problem in Ireland has convinced me that our first step towards its solution is to be found in a better organisation of the farmer's business. It is strange but true that the level of efficiency reached in many European countries was due to American competition, which in the last half of the nineteenth century forced Continental farmers to reorganise their industry alike in production, in distribution and in its finance. Both Irish experience and Continental study have convinced me that neither good husbandry nor a worthy social life can be ensured unless accompanied by intelligent and efficient business methods. We must, therefore, examine somewhat critically the agricultural system of the American farmer, and see wherein its weakness lies.

[Pg 88]

The superiority of the business methods of the town to those of the country is obvious, but I do not think the precise nature of that superiority is generally understood. What strikes the eye is the material apparatus of business,—the street cars, the advertisements, the exchange, the telephone, the typewriter; all these form an impressive contrast with the slow, simple life of the farmer, who very likely scratches his accounts on a shingle or keeps them in his head. But most of this city apparatus is due merely to the necessity of swift movement in the concentrated process of exchange and distribution. Such swiftness is neither necessary nor possible in the process of isolated production. But there is an economic law, applicable alike to rural and to urban pursuits, which is being more and more fully recognised and obeyed by the farmers of most European countries, including Ireland, but which has been too little heeded by the farmers of the United States and Great Britain. Under modern [Pg 89] economic conditions, things must be done in a large way if they are to be done profitably; and this necessitates a resort to combination.

The advantage which combination gives to the town over the country was recognised long before the recent economic changes forced men to combine. In the old towns of Europe all trades began

56

as strict and exclusive corporations. In the eighteenth and nineteenth centuries new scientific and economic forces broke up these
combinations, which were far too narrow for the growing volume of
industrial activity, and an epoch of competition began. The great
towns of America opened their business career during this epoch,
and have brought the arts of competition to a higher perfection than
exists in Europe. But it has always been known that competition did
not exclude combination against the consumer; and it is now beginning to be perceived that the fiercer the competition, the more surely does it lead in the end to such combination.

[Pg 90]

A trade combination has three principal objects: it aims, first, at
improving what I may call the internal business methods of the
trade itself by eliminating the waste due to competition, by econo-
mising staff, plant, etc., and by the ready circulation of intelligence,
and in other ways. In the second place, it aims at strengthening the
trade against outside interests. These may be of various kinds; but
in the typical case we are considering, namely, the combination of
great middlemen who control exchange and distribution, the outside interests are those of the producer on one side and the consumer on the other; and the trade combination, by its organised unity of
action, succeeds in lowering the prices it pays to the unorganised
producer and in raising the prices it charges to the unorganised
consumer. In the third place, the trade combination seeks to favour
its own interests in their relation to other interests through political
control—control not so much of the machinery of politics as of [Pg
91] its products, legislation and administration. I am not now argu-
ing the question whether or how far this action on the part of trade
combinations is morally justifiable. My point is simply that the
towns have flourished at the expense of the country by the use of
these methods, and that the countryman must adopt them if he is to
get his own again. Moreover, as organisation tends to increase the
volume and lower the cost of agricultural production and to make
possible large transactions between organised communities of
farmers and the trade, it will be seen that the organised combination
of farmers will simplify the whole commerce of those countries
where it is adopted, and thus benefit alike the farmer and the trader.

This truth will be easily realised if we consider for a moment the system of distribution which the food demand of the modern market has evolved. Agricultural produce finds its chief market in the great cities. Their populations must have their food so [Pg 92] sent in that it can be rapidly distributed; and this requires that the consignments must be delivered regularly, in large quantities, and of such uniform quality that a sample will give a correct indication of the whole. These three conditions are essential to rapid distribution, but their fulfilment is not within the power of isolated farmers, however large their operations. It is an open question whether farmers should themselves undertake the distribution of their produce through agencies of their own, thus saving the wholesale and possibly the retail profits. But unquestionably they should be so well organised at home that they can take this course if they are unfairly treated by organised middlemen. The Danish farmers, whose highly organised system of distribution has made them the chief competitors of the Irish farmers, have established (with Government assistance which their organisation enabled them to secure) very efficient machinery for distributing their butter, bacon and eggs in [Pg 93] the British markets. Other European farming communities are becoming equally well organised, and similarly control the marketing of their produce. But where, as in America and the United Kingdom, the town dominates the country, and the machinery of distribution is owned by the business men of the towns, it is worked by them in their own interests. They naturally take from the unorganised producers as well as from the unorganised consumers the full business value of the service they render. With the growing cost of living, this has become a matter of urgent importance to the towns. In the cheaper-food campaign which began in the late fall of 1909, voices are heard calling the farmers to account for their uneconomical methods, while here and there organisations of consumers are endeavouring to solve the problem to their own satisfaction by acquiring land and raising upon it the produce which they require.

In the face of such facts it is not easy to [Pg 94] account for the backwardness of American and British farmers in the obviously important matter of organisation. The farmer, we know, is everywhere the most conservative and individualistic of human beings.

He dislikes change in his methods, and he venerates those which have come down to him from his fathers' fathers. Whatever else he may waste, these traditions he conserves. He does not wish to interfere with anybody else's business, and he is fixedly determined that others shall not interfere with his. These estimable qualities make agricultural organisation more difficult in Anglo-Saxon communities than in those where clan or tribal instincts seem to survive. [4]

[Pg 95]

Now it is fair to the farmer to admit that his calling does not lend itself readily to associative action. He lives apart; most of his time is spent in the open air, and in the evening of the working day physical repose is more congenial to him than mental activity. But when all this is said, we have not a complete explanation of the fact that, by failing to combine, American and British farmers, persistently disobey an accepted law, and refuse to follow the almost universal practice of modern business. I believe the true explanation to be one that has somehow escaped the notice of the agricultural economist. Those who accept it will feel that they have found the weak spot in American farming, and that the remedy is neither obscure nor difficult to apply.

The form of combination which the towns have invented for industrial and commercial purposes is the Joint Stock Company. Here a number of persons contribute their capital to a common fund and entrust the direction [Pg 96] to a single head or committee, taking no further part in the business except to change the management if the undertaking does not yield a satisfactory dividend. Our urban way of looking at things has made us assume that this city system must be suitable to rural conditions. The contrary is the fact. When farmers combine, it is a combination not of money only, but of personal effort in relation to the entire business. In a coöperative creamery, for example, the chief contribution of a shareholder is in milk; in a coöperative elevator, corn; in other cases it may be fruit or vegetables, or a variety of material things rather than cash. But it is, most of all, a combination of neighbours within an area small enough to allow of all the members meeting frequently at the business centre. As the system develops, the local associations are federated for larger business transactions, but these are governed by delegates carefully chosen by the members of the constituent bodies.

[Pg 97]

The object of such associations is, primarily, not to declare a dividend, but rather to improve the conditions of the industry for the members. After an agreed interest has been paid upon the shares, the net profits are divided between the participants in the undertaking, to each in proportion as he has contributed to them through the business he has done with the institution. And the same idea is applied to the control of the management. It is recognised that the poor man's coöperation is as important as the rich man's subscription. 'One man, one vote,' is the almost universal principle in coöperative bodies. [5]

The distinction between the capitalistic basis of joint stock organisation and the more human character of the coöperative system is fundamentally important. It is [Pg 98] recognised by law in England, where the coöperative trading societies are organised under *The Industrial and Provident Societies' Act*, and the coöperative credit associations under *The Friendly Societies' Act*. In the United States (I am told by friends in the legal profession), the Articles of Association of an ordinary limited liability company can be so drafted as to meet all the requirements I have named. Most countries have enacted laws specially devised to meet the requirements of coöperative societies. However it is done, the essential of success in agricultural coöperation is that the terms and conditions upon which it is based shall be accepted by all concerned as being equitable in the distribution of profits, risks and control. It then becomes the interest of every member to give his whole-hearted support and aid to the common undertaking. To accomplish this, it is necessary to explain and secure the acceptance of a constitution and procedure carefully thought out to suit each [Pg 99] case. It will be readily believed that associations of farmers which will meet these conditions are not likely to be spontaneously generated; hence the necessity for a plan and for the machinery to carry it through.

In this matter I am here speaking from practical experience in Ireland. Twenty years ago the pioneers of our rural life movement found it necessary to concentrate their efforts upon the reorganisation of the farmer's business. They saw that foreign competition was not, as was commonly supposed, a visitation of Providence upon the farmers of the British Islands, but a natural economic revolution of permanent effect. Our message to Irish farmers was that they must imitate the methods of their Continental competitors, who were defeating them in their own markets simply by superior organisation. After five years of individual propagandism, the Irish Agricultural Organisation Society was formed in 1894 to meet the demand for instruction as to the formation and the [Pg 100] working of coöperative societies, a demand to which it was beyond the means of the few pioneers to respond.

Two decades of steady development have confirmed the soundness of the original scheme, and a brief account of agricultural coöperation in Ireland will be of interest to any reader who has persevered so far. The conditions were in some respects favourable. The farms are small and their owners belong to the class to which coöperation brings most immediate benefit. The Irish peasantry are highly intelligent. They lack the strong individualism of the English, but they have highly developed associative instincts. For this reason coöperation, an alternative to communism,—which they abhor,— comes naturally to them. On the other hand, the ease with which they can be organised makes them peculiarly amenable to political influence. In backward rural communities the trader is almost invariably the political boss. He is a leader of agrarian agitation, [Pg 101] in which he can safely advocate principles he would not like to see applied to the relations between himself and his customers. He bitterly opposes coöperation, which throws inconvenient light upon those relations. We are able to persuade the more enlightened rural traders that economies effected in agricultural production will raise the standard of living of his customers and make them larger consumers of general commodities and more punctual in their payments. But in the majority of cases the agricultural organiser finds politics in sharp conflict with business, and has a hard row to hoe. So, while we have advantages in organising Irish farmers, we have also, largely owing to well-known historical causes, to overcome difficulties which have no counterpart in the United States or England.

Nevertheless, we managed to make progress. We began with the dairying industry, and already half the export of Irish butter comes from the coöperative societies we [Pg 102] established. Organised bodies of farmers are learning to purchase their agricultural requirements intelligently and economically. They are also beginning to adopt the methods of the organised foreign farmer in controlling the sale of their butter, eggs and poultry in the British markets. And they not only combine in agricultural production and distribution, but are also making a promising beginning in grappling with the problem of agricultural finance. It is in this last portion of the Irish programme that by far the most interesting study of the coöperative system can be made, on account of its success in the poorest parts of the Island. Furthermore, the attempt to enable the most embarrassed section of the Irish peasantry to procure working capital illustrates some features of agricultural coöperation which will have suggestive value for American farmers. I will therefore give a brief description of our agricultural coöperative credit associations.

[Pg 103]

The organisation was introduced in the middle of the last century by a German Burgomaster, the now famous Herr Raiffeisen. He set himself to provide the means of escape from the degrading indebtedness to storekeepers and usurers which is the almost invariable lot of poor peasantries. His scheme performs an apparent miracle. A body of very poor persons, individually — in the commercial sense of the term — insolvent, manage to create a new basis of security which has been somewhat grandiloquently and yet truthfully called the capitalisation of their honesty and industry. The way in which this is done is remarkably ingenious. The credit society is organised in the usual democratic way explained above, but its constitution is peculiar in one respect. The members have to become jointly and severally responsible for the debts of the association, which borrows on this unlimited liability from the ordinary commercial bank, or, in some cases, from Government sources. After [Pg 104] the initial stage, when the institution becomes firmly established, it attracts local deposits, and thus the savings of the community, which are too often hoarded, are set free to fructify in the community. The procedure by which the money borrowed is lent to the members of the association is the essential feature of the scheme. The member requiring the loan must state what he is going to do with the money. He must satisfy the committee of the association, who know the man and his business, that the proposed investment is one which will enable him to repay both principal and interest. He must enter into a bond with two sureties for the repayment of the loan, and needless to say the characters of both the borrower and his sureties are very carefully considered. The period for which the loan is granted is arranged to meet the needs of the case, as determined by the committee after a full discussion with the borrower. Once the loan has been made, it becomes the concern of [Pg 105] every member of the association to see that it is applied to the 'approved purpose'—as it is technically called. What is more important is that all the borrower's fellow-members become interested in his business and anxious for its success.

The fact that nearly three hundred of these societies are at work in Ireland, and that, although their transactions are on a very modest scale, the system is steadily growing both in the numbers of its adherents and in the business transacted is, I think, a remarkable testimony to the value of the coöperative system. The details I have given illustrate the important distinction between coöperation, which enables the farmer to do his business in a way that suits him, and the urban form of combination, which is unsuited to his needs. The ordinary banks lend money to agriculturists for a term (generally ninety days) which has been fixed to suit the needs of town business. Thus, a farmer borrowing money to sow a [Pg 106] crop, or to purchase young cattle, is obliged to repay his loan, in the first instance, before the crop is harvested, and in the second, before the cattle mature and are marketable. Far more important, however, than these not inconsiderable economic advantages are the social benefits which are derived by bringing people together to achieve in a very definite and practical way the aim of all coöperative effort—self-help by mutual help.

Our coöperative movement, taken as a whole, is to-day represented by nearly one thousand farmers' organisations, with an aggregate membership of some one hundred thousand persons, mostly heads of families. Its business turnover last year was twelve and a half million dollars. In estimating the significance of these figures, American readers must not 'think in continents,' and must give more weight to the moral than to the material achievement. As I have explained, the coöperative system [Pg 107] requires for its success the exercise of higher moral qualities than does the joint stock company. Once a coöperative society becomes a soulless corporation, its days are numbered. It requires also the diffusion of a good deal of economic thought among its members, and this, also, is no small matter in the conditions. The most striking fact about this work in Ireland is that while in its earlier years organisation consisted mainly in expounding and commending to farmers the coöperative principle, we now find that the principle is taken for granted and the only question upon which advice is needed is how to apply it. The progress of agricultural coöperation depends largely on the character of the community; its commercial value may be measured by the extent to which it develops in the community the mental and moral qualities essential to success. [6]

[Pg 108]

In agricultural coöperation, Ireland can claim to have shown the way to the United Kingdom. Ten years ago, after the Irish movement had been launched, the English rural reformers started a movement on exactly the same lines, even founding on the Irish model an English Agricultural Organisation Society. An Irishman, who had studied coöperation at home, was selected as its chief executive officer. Five years later, a Scottish Agricultural Organisation Society took the field. Both in England and in Scotland the chief difficulty to be overcome is the intense individualism of the farmers, and perhaps some lack of altruism. The large farmers did not feel the need of coöperation, and where the natural leader of the rural community will not lead, the small cultivator cannot follow. Whether the same difficulties have prevented any considerable adoption of agricultural coöperation in the United States, it is not necessary to inquire. It is certain that the underlying principles [Pg 109] approved by every progressive rural, community in Europe have not so far exercised more than an occasional and fitful influence upon the rural economy of the American Republic.

If I have given in these pages a true explanation of the deplorable backwardness of American farmers in the matter of business combination when compared with all other American workers, those who take part in the movement which is to provide the remedy will have set themselves a task as hopeful as it is interesting. Americans as a people are addicted to associated action. I have seen the principle of coöperation developed to the highest point in the ranching industry in the days of the unfenced range. Our cattle used to roam at large, the only means of identifying them being certain registered marks made by the branding-iron and the knife. The individual owner would have had no more property in his herd than he would have had in so many fishes in the sea [Pg 110] but for a very effective coöperative organisation. The Stock Association, with its 'round-ups' and its occasional resort to the Supreme Court of Judge Lynch, were an adequate substitute for the title deeds to the lands, and for fences horse-high, bull-strong and hog-tight. But then we were in the Arid Belt and the frontier-pioneer stage; we had no politics and no politicians. I must return, however, to the less exciting, but I suppose more important, life of the regular farmer, and consider his efforts at organisation.

Instances can be multiplied where the coöperative system has been adopted with immensely beneficial results; but in too many cases it has been abandoned. On the other hand, Granges, Institutes, Clubs, Leagues, Alliances and a multitude of miscellaneous farmers' associations have been organised for social, religious, political and economic objects. From my study of the work done by these bodies, the impression left is that almost everything that can be done better by [Pg 111] working together than by working separately has been at some time the subject of organised effort. But these manifestations of activity have been fitful and sporadic. They were commonly marked by some or all of the same defects—mutual distrust, divided counsels, ignorance of what others were doing, want of continuity and impatience of results. Many organisations, after winning some advantages,—over the railroads for instance,—fell into abeyance or even out of existence; others lapsed under the enervating influence of a little temporary prosperity, such as a few years of better prices. The truth is, American farmers have had the will to organise, but they have missed the way. [7]

The political influence of the farming community has for this reason never been commensurate either with the numerical strength of its members or the magnitude of their [Pg 112] share in the nation's work. It is true that the Federal Department of Agriculture, appropriations for Agricultural Colleges, some railway legislation and other boons to farmers, are to be attributed to the efforts of their organisations. Yet, as compared with the influence exercised upon National affairs by the farmers of, say, France and Denmark, the American farmer has but a small influence upon legislation and administration affecting his interests. What better proof of this could be given than the absence of a Parcels Post in the United States? The whole farming community are agreed as to the need for this boon to the dwellers of the open country, and yet they have not succeeded in winning it against the opposition of the Express Companies, because it is merely a farmers' and not a townsmen's grievance. And not only political impotence, but political inertia, result from the lack of organisation. The state of the country roads—one of the greatest disabilities under which country life in [Pg 113] the United States still suffers—is as good an instance as I know. Congress has shown itself well disposed towards the farmer, but not always so the State governments, and the good intentions of Congress on the roads question are largely nullified owing to the failure of one-third of the States to establish highway commissions, or make other provision for expending such amounts as might be voted to them by Congress. Here, as in the cases of the transit and marketing problems, we see the need for a strong, central, permanent organisation, fitted alike to direct local or promote National action; an association capable of securing the legislative protection of the farmer's interests, and an organisation fitted to further the business side of his industry. In fact, this need is urgent, and a coöperative movement of National dimensions should be established to meet it. Had such a movement been started after the War, or even twenty years later, the American farmer would be in a far stronger position [Pg 114] to-day, and much misdirected effort would have been saved.

I have now tried to explain the weak spot in American rural economy. It may be regarded from a more general point of view. If we were considering the life of some commercial or industrial community and trying to forecast its future development, one of the first things we should note would be its general business methods. No manufacturing concern with a defective office administration and incompetent travellers could survive, even if it had an Archimedes or an Edison in supreme control. I cannot see any reason why an agricultural community should expect to prosper while the industry by which its members live retains its present business organisation. I have urged that as things are, the farming interest is at a fatal disadvantage in the purchase of agricultural requirements, in the sale of agricultural produce, and in obtaining proper credit facilities. Whatever the cause—and I have [Pg 115] set down those which I regard as the chief among them—American farmers have still to learn that they are subject to a law of modern business which governs all their country's industrial activities—the law that each body of workers engaged in supplying the modern market must combine, or be worsted at every turn in competition with those who do.

I do not much fear that this general principle, overlooked, perhaps, because it was too obvious to be worth enforcing, will be disputed. I hope I may gain acceptance for my further contention that the inability of American farmers to sustain an effective business organisation has been due simply to the fact that the not obvious distinction between the capitalistic and the coöperative basis of combination suitable to town and country respectively was missed. For it will then be clear why, in the working out of Mr. Roosevelt's formula, better business must precede and form the basis of better farming [Pg 116] and better living. The conviction that in this general procedure lies the one hope of solving the problem under review accounts for the otherwise disproportionate space given to that aspect of rural life which is of the least interest to the general reader.

I shall now attempt to determine the principles which must be applied to the solution of our problem. Those who have followed the arguments up to this point will have a pretty clear idea of the general drift of my conclusions. The substitution in rural economy of the coöperative for the competitive principle, which I have so far advocated as a matter of business prudence, will be seen to have a wider import. This course will be shown to have an important bearing upon the application of the new knowledge to the oldest industry and also upon the building of a new rural civilisation we must provide for the dwellers of the open country a larger share of the intellectual and social pleasures for the want of which those most needed in the country are too often drawn to the town.

FOOTNOTES:

[4] I should expect the negroes in the Southern States to be very good subjects for agricultural organisation. I have discussed this question with the staff of the Hampton Institute in Virginia—a fine body of men, doing noble work. The Principal, the Rev. H. B. Frissell, D.D., whose judgment in this matter is probably the weightiest in the United States, and his leading assistants, both white and coloured, are of the same opinion.

[5] Where capital is, in rare instances, subscribed by persons other than farmers, it is usually invested less as a commercial speculation than as an act of friendship on the part of the investor, who in no case exercises more control than his one vote affords.

[6] Readers who are sufficiently interested in the rural life movement in Ireland will find a full description of it in my book, "Ireland in the New Century," John Murray, London, and E. P. Dutton, New York.

[7] Mr. John Lee Coulter contributed to the *Yale Review* for November, 1909, an article on Organization among the farmers of the United States which is a most valuable summary of the important facts.

[Pg 119]

CHAPTER VI

THE WAY TO BETTER FARMING AND BETTER LIVING

In no way is the contrast between rural and urban civilisation more marked than in the application of the teachings of modern science to their respective industries. Even the most important mechanical inventions were rather forced upon the farmer by the efficient selling organisation of the city manufacturers than demanded by him as a result of good instruction in farming. On the mammoth wheat farms, where, as the fable ran, the plough that started out one morning returned on the adjoining furrow the following day, mechanical science was indeed called in, but only to perpetrate the greatest soil robbery in agricultural history. Application of science to legitimate agriculture is [Pg 120] comparatively new. In my ranching and farming days I well remember how general was the disbelief in its practical value throughout the Middle and Far West. In cowboy terminology, all scientists were classified as "bug-hunters," and farmers generally had no use for the theorist. The non-agricultural community had naturally no higher appreciation of the farmer's calling than he himself displayed. When some Universities first developed agricultural courses, the students who entered for them were nicknamed "aggies," and were not regarded as adding much to the dignity of a seat of higher learning. The Department of Agriculture was looked upon as a source of jobs, graft being the nearest approach to any known agricultural operation.

All this is changing fast. The Federal Department of Agriculture is now perhaps the most popular and respected of the world's great administrative institutions. In the Middle West, a newly awakened public [Pg 121] opinion has set up an honourable rivalry between such States as Wisconsin, Iowa, Illinois, Nebraska and Minnesota, in developing the agricultural sides of their Universities and Colleges. None the less, Mr. James J. Hill has recently given it as his opinion that not more than one per cent of the farmers of these regions are working in direct touch with any educational institution. It is probable that this estimate leaves out of account the indirect influence of the vast amount of extension work and itinerant instruction which is embraced in the activities of the Universities and Colleges. I fear it cannot be denied that in the application of the natural sciences to the practical, and of economic science to the business of farming, the country folk are decades behind their urban fellow-citizens. And again I say the disparity is to be attributed to the difference in their respective degrees of organisation for business purposes.

The relation between business [Pg 122] organisation and economic progress ought, I submit, to be very seriously considered by the social workers who perceive that progress is mainly a question of education. Speaking from administrative experience at home, and from a good deal of interested observation in America, I am firmly convinced that the new rural education is badly handicapped by the lack of organised bodies of farmers to act as channels for the new knowledge now made available. In some instances, I am aware, great good has been done by the formation of farmers' institutes which have been established in order to interest rural communities in educational work and to make the local arrangements for instruction by lectures, demonstrations and otherwise. But all European experience proves the superiority for this purpose of the business association to the organisation *ad hoc*, and has a much better chance of permanence.

Again, the influence upon rural life of the agricultural teaching of the Colleges and [Pg 123] Universities, as exercised by their pupils, may be too easily accepted as being of greater potential utility than any work which these institutions can do amongst adults. This is a mistake. The thousands of young men who are now being trained for advanced farming too often have to restrict the practical application of their theoretic knowledge to the home circle, which is not always responsive, for a man is not usually a prophet in his own family. It is here that the educational value of coöperative societies comes in; they act as agencies through which scientific teaching may become actual practice, not in the uncertain future, but in the living present. A coöperative association has a quality which should commend it to the social reformer—the power of evoking character; it brings to the front a new type of local leader, not the best talker, but the man whose knowledge enables him to make some solid contribution to the welfare of the community.

I come now to the last part of the threefold [Pg 124] scheme—that which aims at a better life upon the farm. The coöperative association, in virtue of its non-capitalistic basis of constitution and procedure (which, as I have explained, distinguishes it from the Joint Stock Company), demands as a condition of its business success the exercise of certain social qualities of inestimable value to the community life. It is for this reason, no doubt, that where men and women have learned to work together under this system in the business of their lives, they are easily induced to use their organisation for social and intellectual purposes also.

The new organisation of the rural community for social as well as economic purposes, which should follow from the acceptance of the opinion I have advanced, would bring with it the first effective counter-attraction to the towns. Their material advantages the country cannot hope to rival; nor can any conceivable evolution of rural life furnish a real counterpart to the cheap and garish [Pg 125] entertainments of the modern city. Take, for example, the extravagant use of electric light for purposes of advertisement, which affords a nightly display of fireworks in any active business street of an American city far superior to the occasional exhibition at the Crystal Palace in London, which was the rare treat of my childhood days. These delights—if such they be—cannot be extended into remote villages in Kansas or Nebraska; but their enchantment must be reckoned with by those who would remould the life of the open country and make it morally and mentally satisfying to those who are born to it, or who, but for its social stagnation, would prefer a rural to an urban existence.

In one of his many public references to country life, President Roosevelt attributed the rural exodus to the desire of "the more active and restless young men and women" to escape from "loneliness and lack of mental companionship." [8] He is hopeful [Pg 126] that the rural free delivery, the telephone, the bicycle and the trolley will do much towards "lessening the isolation of farm life and making it brighter and more attractive." Many to whom I have spoken on this subject fear that the linking of the country with the town by these applications of modern science may, to some extent, operate in a direction the opposite of that which Mr. Roosevelt anticipates and desires. According to this view, the more intimate knowledge of the modern city may increase the desire to be in personal touch with it; the telephone may fail to give through the ear the satisfaction which is demanded by the eye; among the "more active and restless young men and women" the rural free delivery may circulate the dime novel and the trolley make accessible the dime museum. In the total result the occasional visit may become more and more frequent, until the duties of country life are first neglected and then abandoned.

[Pg 127]

I do not feel competent to decide between these two views, but I offer one consideration with which I think many rural reformers will agree. The attempt to bring the advantages of the city within the reach of the dwellers in the country cannot, of itself, counteract the townward tendency in so far as it is due to the causes summarised above. However rapidly, in this respect, the country may be improved, the city is sure to advance more rapidly and the gap between them to be widened. The new rural civilisation should aim at trying to develop in the country the things of the country, the very existence of which seems to have been forgotten. But, after all, it is the world within us rather than the world without us that matters in the making of society, and I must give to the social influence of the coöperative idea what I believe to be its real importance.

In Ireland, from which so much of my experience is drawn, we have found a tendency growing among farmers whose combinations [Pg 128] are successful, to gather into one strong local association all those varied objects and activities which I have described as advocated by the Irish Agricultural Organisation Society. These local associations are ceasing to have one special purpose or one object only. They absorb more and more of the business of the district. One large, well-organised institution is being substituted for the numerous petty transactions of farmers with middlemen and small country traders. Gradually the Society becomes the most important institution in the district, the most important in a social as well as in an economic sense. The members feel a pride in its material expansion. They accumulate large profits, which in time become a kind of communal fund. In some cases this is used for the erection of village halls where social entertainments, concerts and dances are held, lectures delivered and libraries stored. Finally, the association assumes the character of a rural commune, where, instead of the old [Pg 129] basis of the commune, the joint ownership of land, a new basis for union is found in the voluntary communism of effort.

A true social organism is thus being created with common human and economic interests, and the clan feeling, which was so powerful an influence in early and mediæval civilisations, with all its power of generating passionate loyalties, is born anew in the modern world. Our ancient Irish records show little clans with a common ownership of land hardly larger than a parish, but with all the patriotic feeling of large nations held with an intensity rare in our modern states. The history of these clans and of very small nations like the ancient Greek states shows that the social feeling assumes its most binding and powerful character where the community is large enough to allow free play to the various interests of human life, but is not so large that it becomes an abstraction to the imagination. Most of us feel no greater thrill in being one of a State with fifty million inhabitants than [Pg 130] we do in recognising we are citizens of the solar system. The rural commune and the very small States exhibit the feeling of human solidarity in its most intense manifestations, working on itself, regenerating itself and seeking its own perfection. Combinations of agriculturists, when the rural organisation is complete, re-create in a new way the conditions where these social instincts germinate best, and it is only by this complete organisation of rural life that we can hope to build up a rural civilisation, and create those counter-attractions to urban life which will stay the exodus from the land.

I do not wish to exaggerate the interest which the rural life of my own little island may have for those who are concerned for the vast and wealthy expanses of the American farm lands. But, even here there is a genuine desire for the really simple life, which in its commonest manifestation is a thing that rather simple people talk about. In a properly organised rural [Pg 131] neighbourhood could be developed that higher kind of attraction which is suggested by the very word *neighbourhood*. Once get the farmers and their families all working together at something that concerns them all, and we have the beginning of a more stable and a more social community than is likely to exist amid the constant change and bustle of the large towns, where indeed some thinkers tell us that not only the family, but also the social life, is badly breaking down. When people are really interested in each other—and this interest comes of habitually working together—the smallest personal traits or events affecting one are of interest to all. The simplest piece of amateur acting or singing, done in the village hall by one of the villagers, will arouse more criticism and more enthusiasm among his friends and neighbours than can be excited by the most consummate performance of a professional in a great city theatre, where no one in the audience knows or cares for the performer.

[Pg 132]

But if this attraction—the attraction of common work and social intercourse with a circle of friends—is to prevail in the long run over the lure which the city offers to eye and ear and pocket, there must be a change in rural education. At present country children are educated as if for the purpose of driving them into the towns. To the pleasure which the cultured city man feels in the country—because he has been taught to feel it—the country child is insensible. The country offers continual interest to the mind which has been trained to be thoughtful and observant; the town offers continual distraction to the vacant eye and brain. Yet, the education given to country children has been invented for them in the town, and it not only bears no relation to the life they are to lead, but actually attracts them towards a town career. I am aware that I am here on ground where angels—even if specialised in pedagogy—may well fear to tread. Upon the principles of a sound [Pg 133] agricultural education pedagogues are in a normally violent state of disagreement with each other. But whatever compromise between general education and technical instruction be adopted, the resulting reform that is needed has two sides. We want two changes in the rural mind— beginning with the rural teacher's mind. First, the interest which the physical environment of the farmer provides to followers of almost every branch of science must be communicated to the agricultural classes according to their capacities. Second, that intimacy with and affection for nature, to which Wordsworth has given the highest expression, must in some way be engendered in the rural mind. In this way alone will the countryman come to realize the beauty of the life around him, as through the teaching of science he will learn to realise its truth.

Upon this reformed education, as a basis, the rural economy must be built. It must, if my view be accepted, ensure, first and foremost, the combination of farmers for [Pg 134] business purposes in such a manner as will enable them to control their own marketing and make use of the many advantages which a command of capital gives. In all European countries—with the exception of the British Isles—statesmen have recognised the national necessity for the good business organisation of the farmer. In some cases, for example France, even Government officials expound the coöperative principle. In Denmark, the most predominantly rural country in Europe, the education both in the common and in the high school has long been so admirably related to the working lives of the agricultural classes that the people adopt spontaneously the methods of organisation which the commercial instinct they have acquired through education tells them to be suitable to the conditions. The rural reformer knows that this is the better way; but our problem is not merely the education of a rising, but the development of a grown-up generation. We cannot wait [Pg 135] for the slow process of education to produce its effect upon the mind of the rural youth, even if there were any way of ensuring their proper training for a progressive rural life without first giving to their parents such education as they can assimilate. Direct action is called for; we have to work with adult farmers and induce them to reorganise their business upon the lines which I have attempted to define. Moreover, this is essential to the future success of the work done in the schools, in order that the trained mind of youth may not afterwards find itself baulked by the ignorant apathy or lazy conservatism of its elders.

I hold, then, that the new economy will mean a more scientific mastery of the technical side of farming, for farmers will make a much larger use of the advice, instruction and help which the Nation and the States offer them through the Department of Agriculture and the Colleges. It is equally certain that there will arise a more human [Pg 136] social life in the rural districts, based upon the greater share of the products of the farmer's industry, which the new business organisation will enable him to retain; stimulated by the closer business relations with his fellows which that organisation will bring about, and fostered by the closer neighbourhood which is implied in a more intensive cultivation.

The development of a more intensive cultivation must carry with it a much more careful consideration of the labour problem. The difficulty of getting and keeping labour on the farm is a commonplace. I think farmers have not faced the fact that this difficulty is due in the main to their own way of doing their business. Competent men will not stay at farm labour unless it offers them continuous employment as part of a well-ordered business concern; and this is not possible unless with a greatly improved husbandry.

To-day agriculture has to compete in the [Pg 137] labour market against other, and to many men more attractive, industries, and a marked elevation in the whole standard of life in the rural world is the best insurance of a better supply of good farm labour. Only an intensive system of farming can afford any large amount of permanent employment at decent wages to the rural labourer, and only a good supply of competent labour can render intensive farming on any large scale practicable. But the intensive system of farming not only gives regular employment and good wages; it also fits the labourer of to-day—in a country where a man can strike out for himself—to be the successful farmer of to-morrow. Nor, in these days of impersonal industrial relations, should the fact be overlooked that under an intensive system of agriculture, we find still preserved the kindly personal relation between employer and employed which contributes both to the pleasantness of life and to economic progress and security.

[Pg 138]

Moreover, in a country where advanced farming is the rule, there is a remarkable, and, from the standpoint of national stability, most valuable, steadiness in employment. Good farming, by fixing the labourer on the soil, improves the general condition of rural life, by ridding the countryside of the worst of its present pests. Those wandering dervishes of the industrial world, the hobo, the tramp— the entire family of Weary Willies and Tired Timothys—will no longer have even an imaginary excuse for their troubled and troublesome existence. But the farmer who was the prey of these pests must, if he would be permanently rid of them, learn to respect his hired farm hand. He must provide him with a comfortable cottage and a modest garden plot upon which his young family may employ themselves; otherwise, whatever the farmer may do to attract labour, he will never retain it. In short, the labourer, too, must get his full and fair share of the prosperity of the coming good time in the country.

[Pg 139]

There is one particular aspect of this improved social life which is so important that it ought properly to form the subject of a separate essay; I mean the position of women in rural life. In no country in the world is the general position of woman better, or her influence greater, than in the United States. But while woman has played a great part there in the social life and economic development of the town, I hold that the part she is destined to play in the future making of the country will be even greater.

In the more intelligent scheme of the new country life, the economic position of woman is likely to be one of high importance. She enters largely into all three parts of our programme,—better farming, better business, better living. In the development of higher farming, for instance, she is better fitted than the more muscular but less patient animal, man, to carry on with care that work of milk records, egg records, etc., which underlies the selection on scientific lines of the more [Pg 140] productive strains of cattle and poultry. And this kind of work is wanted in the study not only of animal, but also of plant life.

Again, in the sphere of better business, the housekeeping faculty of woman is an important asset, since a good system of farm accounts is one of the most valuable aids to successful farming. But it is, of course, in the third part of the programme,—better living,—that woman's greatest opportunity lies. The woman makes the home life of the Nation. But she desires also social life, and where she has the chance she develops it. Here it is that the establishment of the coöperative society, or union, gives an opening and a range of conditions in which the social usefulness of woman makes itself quickly felt. I do not think that I am laying too much stress on this matter, because the pleasures, the interests and the duties of society, properly so called,—that is, the state of living on friendly terms with our neighbours,—are always more central and [Pg 141] important in the life of a woman than of a man. The man needs them, too, for without them he becomes a mere machine for making money; but the woman, deprived of them, tends to become a mere drudge. The new rural social economy (which implies a denser population occupying smaller holdings) must therefore include a generous provision for all those forms of social intercourse which specially appeal to women. The Women's Sections of the Granges have done a great deal of useful work in this direction; we need a more general and complete application of the principles on which they act.

I have now stated the broad principles which must govern any effective scheme for correcting the present harmful subordination of rural life to a civilisation too exclusively urban. Before I bring forward my definite proposal for a remedy calculated to meet the needs of the situation, I must anticipate a line of criticism which may occur to the mind of any social worker who [Pg 142] does not happen to be very familiar with the conditions of country life.

I can well imagine readers who have patiently followed my arguments wishing to interrogate me in some such terms as these: "Assuming," they may say, "that we accept all you tell us about the neglect of the rural population, and agree as to the grave consequences which must follow if it be continued, what on earth can we do? Of course the welfare of the rural population is a matter of paramount importance to the city and to the nation at large; but may we remind you that you said the evil and the consequences can be removed and averted only by those immediately concerned—the actual farmers—and that the remedy for the rural backwardness was to be sought for in the rural mind? 'Canst thou minister to a mind diseased?' Must not the patient 'minister' to himself?"

Fair questions these, and altogether to the point. I answer at once that the patient [Pg 143] ought to minister to himself, but he won't. He has acquired the habit of sending for the physician of the town, whose physic but aggravates the disease. Dropping metaphor, the farmer does not think for himself. In rural communities, there is as great a lack of collective thought as of coöperative action. All progress is conditional on public opinion, and this, even in the country, is a very much town-made thing.

So I am, then, in this difficulty. My subject is rural, my audience urban. I have to commend to the statesmen and the philanthropists of the town the somewhat incongruous proposal that they should take the initiative in rural reform. Neither the thought nor the influence which can set in motion what in agricultural communities is no less than an economic revolution are to be found in the open country. To the townsmen I now address my appeal and submit a plan.

FOOTNOTE:

[8] Message to the Fifty-eighth Congress (1903).

[Pg 147]

CHAPTER VII

THE TWO THINGS NEEDFUL

In my earlier chapters I traced to the Industrial Revolution in England the origin of that subordination, in the English-speaking countries, of rural to urban interests which finds its expression to-day in the problem of rural life. I have shown that the continuance of the tendency in America was natural if not inevitable, and have urged that, for economic, social and political reasons, its further progress should now be stayed. If my view as to the origin, present effects and probable consequences of the evil be accepted, any serious proposals for a remedy will be welcomed by all who realise that national well-being cannot endure if urban prosperity is accompanied by rural decay. In this belief I offer the scheme for a Country Life movement which has slowly matured in [Pg 148] my own mind as the result of the experience described in the preceding pages.

The first aim of the movement should be to coördinate, and guide towards a common end, the efforts of a large number of agencies—educational, religious, social and philanthropic—which, in their several ways, are already engaged upon some part of the work to be done. For such a movement the United States offers advantages not to be found elsewhere in the area for which we are concerned. For here public-spirited individuals and associations of the kind required exist in larger numbers than can be known to any one who has not watched what is going on in this field of social service. If I had not already devoted too much space to personal experiences, I could of my own knowledge testify to the remarkable growth of organised effort in American rural communities. Sometimes this is the outcome of a growing spirit of neighbourliness, sometimes it emanates from young Universities and Colleges [Pg 149] emulating the extension work with which nearly every big city is familiar. I have been much struck with the way in which, at gatherings of school teachers, pedagogic detail and questions affecting their status and emoluments have become less popular subjects for discussion than schemes of social progress. [9] Similarly, the agricultural Press is becoming less exclusively technical and commercial, and more human. Even the syndicated stuff is getting less townified. My correspondence, newspaper clippings sent to me, and many other indications, point in the same direction. They leave the impression upon my mind that there is a vast, efficient and enthusiastic army of social workers upon the farm lands of the United States badly in need of a Headquarters Staff.

[Pg 150]

If I am right in believing that, of the English-speaking countries, the United States affords the best opportunity for such a consummation, most assuredly the present time is peculiarly auspicious. If Mr. Roosevelt's Country Life policy has not been received with any marked enthusiasm, American public opinion has been thoroughly aroused upon his Conservation policy. The latter cannot possibly come to fruition—nor even go much further—until the Country Life problem is boldly faced. In the Conference of Governors it was pointed out over and over again that the farmer, now the chief waster, must become the chief conserver. As such he will himself become a supporter of the policy, and will bring to the aid of those advocates of Conservation whose chief concern is for future generations, an interested public opinion which will go far to outweigh the influence of those who profit by the exhaustion of natural resources. To the country life reformer I would say that, as the one idea [Pg 151] has caught on while the other lags, he will, if he is wise, hitch his Country Life waggon to the Conservation star.

With every advantage of time and place, the promotion of the movement which is to counteract the townward tendency will have to reckon with the psychological difficulty inherent in the conditions. They must recognise the paradox of the situation already pointed out, the necessity of interesting the town in the problems of the country. The urban attitude of mind which caused the evil, and now makes it difficult to interest public opinion in the remedy, is not new; it pervades the literature of the Augustan age. I recall from my school days Virgil's great handbook on Italian agriculture, written with a mastery of technical detail unsurpassed by Kipling. But the farmers he had in mind when he indulged in his memorable rhapsody upon the happiness of their lot were out for pleasure rather than profit. While the suburban poet sang to the merchant princes, [Pg 152] Rome was paying a bonus upon imported corn, and entering generally upon that fatal disregard for the interest of the rural population which is one of the accepted causes of the decline and fall.

How that Old World tragi-comedy comes back to me when I talk to New York friends on the subject of these pages! I am not, so they tell me, up to date in my information; there is a marked revulsion of feeling upon the town *versus* country question; the tide of the rural exodus has really turned, as I might have discerned without going far afield. At many a Long Island home I might see on Sundays, weather permitting, the horny-handed son of week-day toil in Wall Street, rustically attired, inspecting his Jersey cows and aristocratic fowls. These supply a select circle in New York with butter and eggs, at a price which leaves nothing to be desired—unless it be some information as to the cost of production. Full justice is done to the new country life when the [Pg 153] Farmers' Club of New York fulfils its chief function, the annual dinner at Delmonico's. Then agriculture is extolled in fine Virgilian style, the Hudson villa and the Newport 'cottage' being permitted to divide the honours of the rural revival with the Long Island home. But to my bucolic intelligence, it would seem that against the 'back to the land' movement of Saturday afternoon the captious critic might set the rural exodus of Monday morning.

These reflections are introduced in no unfriendly spirit, and with serious intent. To me this new rural life is associated with memories of characteristically American hospitality; but my interest in it is more than personal. It is giving to those who cultivate it, among whom are the helpers most needed at the moment, a point of view which will enable them to grasp the real problem of the open country, as it exists, for example, in the great food-producing and cotton-growing tracts of the West and South. Both in the [Pg 154] countries where the townward tendency of the industrial age was foreseen and prevented, and in those in which the evil is being cured, the impulse and inspiration which will be required to initiate and sustain our Country Life movement came mainly from leaders who were not themselves agriculturists. [10] Proficiency in the practice or even in the business of farming is not necessary. What is needed is a comprehensive knowledge of public affairs, political imagination, an understanding sympathy with and a philosophic insight into the entire life of communities. Men who combine with the necessary experience those gifts of heart and mind which go to make the higher citizenship in the many, and the statesmanship in the few, will more likely be found in the city than in the country. Yet they are, in the conditions, the natural leaders of the Country Life movement, which must now be defined.

[Pg 155]

The situation demands two things; on the one hand an association, popular, propagandist, organising; on the other, an Institute, scientific, philosophic, research-making. These two things are distinct in character, but they are complementary to each other. One will require popular enthusiasm and business organisation. To the service of the other must be brought the patient spirit of scientific and philosophic analysis and inquiry. These two bodies — the popular propagandist association and the scientific research-making Institute — must, therefore, be created; and, for a reason to be explained when we consider the work of the Institute, they should be independent of each other. This rough indication of the character of the work, which I will describe more in detail presently, will suffice for the moment. I feel that the work will be so intensely human in its interest that it will be well to say at once how the two central agencies can be established, and the movement made, not a [Pg 156] writer's fancy, but a living and doing agency of human progress.

A body, in many respects ideally fitted to give the necessary impulse and direction to the work of organisation, is already in the field. The leaders of the Conservation idea, recognising that their policy, in common with other policies, will need an organised public opinion at its back, have founded a National Conservation Association. Mr. Gifford Pinchot has now been selected as its President. Before he was available, the task of organising and setting to work the new institution was unanimously entrusted to and accepted by President Eliot, of whose qualifications all I will say is that we foreign students of social problems vie with his own countrymen in our appreciation of his public work and aims. These two appointments are sufficient proof of the serious importance of the work, and bespeak public influence and support for the Association. I have no doubt that this body [Pg 157] would be fully qualified to formulate and initiate the Country Life movement, and act as the central agency for the active promotion of its objects. Its members, who, I am sure, agree with Mr. Roosevelt in regarding the movement as a necessary complement to the Conservation policy, might even feel that for this very reason it was incumbent upon them to set their organisation to this work.

There is, however, one consideration which will make Mr. Pinchot and his associates hesitate to adopt this course. The doubt relates to the distinction I have drawn between the Conservation policy and the Country Life movement, the one seeking to promote legislative and administrative action, and the other, while it may give birth to a policy, being chiefly concerned with voluntary effort. [11] Although the National Conservation Association is founded for the purpose of educating public opinion upon the Conservation idea, it may decide to support [Pg 158] the Conservation policy of one party rather than that of another. It would thus become too much involved in party controversy to act as a central agency of a movement which must embrace men of all parties. Should this view prevail, the difficulty can be easily surmounted by following the Irish precedent, where we had a very similar and indeed far more delicate situation to save from political trouble. An American Agricultural Organisation Society could be founded for the purpose in view, and as it is probable that leading advocates of the Conservation policy would take a prominent part in the Country Life movement, the interdependence of the two ideas would have practical recognition.

Apart from the possibility of political complications, there is one strong reason to recommend this course. The movement will accomplish its best and most permanent results as an advocate of self-reliance; it will seek to make self-help effective through [Pg 159] organisation; it will concern itself much more for those things which the farmers can do for themselves by coöperation than with those things which the Government can do for them. [12] The selection, however, between the two alternative courses is a question which the foreign critic cannot decide. The work to which I now return will be the same, whatever agency is charged with its execution.

[Pg 160]

The central body (which for brevity I will call the Association) will have as its general aim the economic and social development of rural communities. The work will be mainly that of active organisation. For reasons explained in the earlier chapters, the organisation must be coöperative in character, and will be concentrated upon the business methods of the farmers. This will, it is believed, cure a radical defect in their system—a defect which, as I have argued, is responsible for a restricted production, and for a course of distribution injurious alike to producer and consumer, besides exercising a depressing influence upon the economic efficiency and social life of rural communities. It follows that the first step towards a general reconstruction of country life, which has the promise of giving to the country a social attraction strong enough to stem the tide of the townward migration, is agricultural coöperation.

Such being the general aim and the [Pg 161] definite procedure, the first practical question that arises will be, how to apply this solvent—agricultural coöperation. It will not suffice to throw these two long words at the hardy rustic; shorter and more emphatic words might come back. Two equally necessary things must be done; the principle must be made clear, and the practical details of this rural equivalent of urban business combination must be explained in language understanded of the people. It is not difficult to draft a paper scheme for this purpose, but the fitting of the plan to local conditions is a very expert business. Hence the central agency should have at its disposal a corps of experts in coöperative organisation for agricultural purposes. After a short visit to a likely district by a competent exponent of the theory and practice, local volunteers would be found to carry on the work. Experience shows that once a well-organised coöperative association of farmers is permanently established, similar associations [Pg 162] spring up spontaneously under the magic influence of proved success in known conditions. I should strongly recommend concentration at first on a few selected districts, with the aim of making standard models to which other communities could work. I need hardly say that all this work would be done in coöperation with whatever other agencies would lend their aid. The Country Life movement would be extremely useful to the great educational foundations centred in New York. I happen to know that the Trustees of the Rockefeller, Carnegie and Russell Sage endowments are keenly desirous to promote such a redirection of rural education as will bring it into a more helpful relation with the working lives of the rural population. Then there are such bodies as the Y. M. C. A., whose leaders, I am told, are alive to the value of the open air life, and are anxious to extend their country work in the rural districts. The great army of rural teachers, the Farmers' Union, and other [Pg 163] farmers' organisations I have already named would gladly coöperate with schemes making for rural progress.

More important, I believe, than is generally realised, from an economic and social point of view, are the rural churches. In many European countries, where agricultural coöperation has played a great part in the people's lives, the clergy have ardently supported the system on account of its moral value. In Ireland, some of our very best volunteer organisers are clergymen. Some leaders of the rural church in the United States have told me that a feeling is growing that an increased economic usefulness in the clergy would strengthen their position in the society which they serve in a higher capacity. I know that the suggestion of clerical intervention in secular affairs is open to misunderstanding. But here is a body of educated citizens who would gladly take part in any real social service; and here is a situation where there is work of high moral [Pg 164] and social value calling for volunteers. Nothing but good, it seems to me, could result if such men, who have more opportunity and inclination for general reading than the working farmer, would help in explaining the intricacies of coöperative organisation and procedure which must be understood and practised in order that the system may be fruitful.

In addition to its active propagandist work, the central Association could exercise a powerful and helpful influence in other ways. It should, of course, keep both the agricultural and the general press informed of its plans and progress. It should also keep in touch with the agricultural work of all important educational bodies, and more especially urge upon them the necessity of spreading the coöperative idea. The Department of Agriculture would welcome and support the movement; for I know many leading men in that service who thoroughly understand and recognise the immense [Pg 165] importance, especially to backward rural communities, of the coöperative principle.

It is not necessary, at this stage, to go further into details. I feel confident that the work of assisting all suitable agencies, such as those I have named, and others which may be available, through organisers of agricultural coöperation and by the spreading of information, would soon enable the central body to render inestimable service to the cause of rural progress. Such, at any rate, is the outline of my first proposal for giving to my American fellow-workers upon the rural problem the assistance which I feel they most need at the present moment. I pass now to my second proposal.

I suggest that an institution—which, as I have said, will be scientific, philosophic, research-making—should be founded. It would be, in effect, a Bureau of research in rural social economy. Personally I know that, in my own experience as an administrator and organiser, I have been constantly [Pg 166] brought face to face with problems where we could turn to no guide—no patient band of investigators who had been measuring, analysing, determining the data. Yet in some directions much excellent work is being done. Every social worker knows how the knowledge of what others are doing will help him. It is strange how little the problems of the rural population have entered into the studies of economists and sociologists. At leading Universities I have sought in vain for light. At a recent anniversary in New York, which brought together the foremost economists of the Old and New World, there was an almost complete omission of the country side of things from a programme which I am sure was generally held to be almost exhaustive. The fact is, the subject must be treated as a new one, and it is urgently necessary, if the work of the Country Life movement is to be based on a solid foundation of fact, to make good the deficiency of information which has resulted from the [Pg 167] general lack of interest in the subject under review. An Institute is wanted to survey the field, to collect, classify and coördinate information and to supplement and carry forward the work of research and inquiry. The rural social worker requires as far as possible to carry exact statistical method into his work so that he may no longer have to depend on general statements, but may have at his command evidence, the validity of which can be trusted, while its significance can be measured. I may mention a few typical questions on which useful light would be shed by the Institute's researches: —

1. The influence of coöperative methods (*a*) on the productive and distributive efficiency of rural communities, and (*b*) on the development of a social country life.

2. The systems of rural education, both general and technical, in different countries, and the administrative and financial basis of each system.

[Pg 168]

3. The relation between agricultural economy and the cost of food.

4. The changes (*a*) in the standard and cost of living, and (*b*) in the economy, solvency and stability of rural communities.

5. The economic interdependence of the agricultural producer and the urban consumer, and the extent and incidence of middle profits in the distribution of agricultural produce.

6. The action taken by different Governments to assist the development and secure the stability of the agricultural classes, and the possibilities and the dangers of such action, with special reference to the delimitation of the respective spheres of State aid and voluntary effort.

7. How far agricultural and rural employment can relieve the problems of city unemployment, and assist the work of social reclamation.

Some may think that I am assigning to two bodies work which could be as well done [Pg 169] by one. While all proposals for multiplying organisations in the field of social service should be critically examined, there are strong reasons in this case for the course I suggest. The two bodies, while working to a common end, will differ essentially in their scope and method. The propagandist agency will be executive and administrative, and while its operations would have suggestive value to the country social worker everywhere, it would be concerned directly only with the United States. Furthermore, it need not necessarily have any lengthened existence as a national propagandist agency. It would be founded mainly to introduce that method into American agricultural economy which I have tried to show lies at the root of rural progress. As soon as the soundness of the general scheme had been demonstrated in any State, the central body would promote an organisation to take over the work within that State. The State organisation would, in its turn, soon be able to [Pg 170] devolve its propagandist work upon a federation of the business associations which it had been the means of establishing. That is the contemplated evolution of my first proposal—the early delegation of the functions of the national to the State propagandist agency, which would further devolve the work upon bodies of farmers organised primarily for economic purposes, but with the ulterior aim of social advancement.

The Country Life Institute would be on a wholly different footing. Its researches, if only to subserve the Country Life movement in the United States, would have to range over the civilised world, and to be historical as well as contemporary. It should be regarded as a contribution to the welfare of the English-speaking peoples, one aspect of whose civilisation—if there be truth in what I have written—needs to be reconsidered in the light which the Institute is designed to afford. Its task will be of no [Pg 171] ephemeral character. Its success will not, as in the case of the active propagandist body, lessen the need for its services, but will rather stimulate the demand for them.

These differences will have to be taken into account in considering the important question of ways and means. Both bodies will, I hope, appeal successfully to public-spirited philanthropists. The temporary body will need only temporary support; perhaps provision for a five-years' campaign would suffice. In the near future, local organisations would naturally defray the cost of the services rendered to them by the central body; but the Country Life Institute would need a permanent endowment. The man fitted for its chief control will not be found idle, but will have to be taken from other work. The scheme, as I have worked it out, will involve prolonged economic and social inquiry over a wide field. This would be conducted mostly by postgraduate students. From those who did this outside [Pg 172] work with credit would be recruited the small staff which would be needed at the central office to get into the most accessible form the facts and opinions which are needed for the guidance of those who are doing practical work in the field of rural regeneration. My estimate of the amount required to do the work well is from forty to fifty thousand dollars a year, or say a capital sum of from a million to a million and a quarter dollars. Whether the project is worthy of such an expenditure, depends upon the question whether I have made good my case.

Let me summarise this case. I have tried to show that modern civilisation is one-sided to a dangerous degree—that it has concentrated itself in the towns and left the country derelict. This tendency is peculiar to the English-speaking communities, where the great industrial movement has had as its consequence the rural problem I have examined. If the townward tendency cannot be checked, it will ultimately bring about the decay of [Pg 173] the towns themselves, and of our whole civilisation, for the towns draw their supply of population from the country. Moreover, the waste of natural resources, and possibly the alarming increase in the price of food, which have lately attracted so much attention in America, are largely due to the fact that those who cultivate the land do not intend to spend their lives upon it; and without a rehabilitation of country life there can be no success for the Conservation policy. Therefore, the Country Life movement deals with what is probably the most important problem before the English-speaking peoples at this time. Now the predominance of the towns which is depressing the country is based partly on a fuller application of modern physical science, partly on superior business organisation, partly on facilities for occupation and amusement; and if the balance is to be redressed, the country must be improved in all three ways. There must be better farming, better business, and better living. These three are [Pg 174] equally necessary, but better business must come first. For farmers, the way to better living is coöperation, and what coöperation means is the chief thing the American farmer has to learn.

FOOTNOTES:

[9] In the capital of Virginia, to take one notable example, I have witnessed a perfect ferment of social activity at one of the gatherings. It brought together such an ideal combination of the best spirits in both rural and urban life that I anticipate some striking developments in rural civilization which will surely extend beyond the borders of the State.

[10] I may mention Raiffeisen, Luzzati, Rocquigny, Bishop Grundtwig, Henry W. Wolff, the Rev. T. A. Finlay, S.J., and most of the leaders in agricultural organization in Great Britain and Ireland.

[11] See above, page 31.

[12] It may seem a small matter even for a footnote, but an unambiguous terminology is so important to propagandist work that I must mention a somewhat unfortunate use of the word 'coöperation' which prevails in official and pedagogic circles. We hear of coöperative demonstration work, coöperative education, coöperative lectures, and so forth. Whenever a Government or State department, or an educational body works with any other agency, and sometimes when they are only doing their own work, they use the term, which is of course grammatically applicable whenever two people work together—from matrimony down. If the word in connection with agriculture could be retained for its technical sense, so long established and well understood in Europe, the proposed movement might be saved a good deal of confused thinking. Might not Government and educational authorities substitute the word 'coördinated' so as to preserve the distinction?

Printed in the United States of America.